Augsburg College
George Sverdrup Library
Minneapolis, Minnesota 55404

THE RISE OF URBAN AMERICA

ADVISORY EDITOR
Richard C. Wade
PROFESSOR OF AMERICAN HISTORY
UNIVERSITY OF CHICAGO

SOLID FOR MULHOOLY

A POLITICAL SATIRE

Rufus E. Shapley

ARNO PRESS
&
The New York Times

NEW YORK • 1970

Reprint Edition 1970 by Arno Press Inc.

Reprinted from a copy in The University of Chicago Library

LC# 76-112572
ISBN 0-405-02475-4

THE RISE OF URBAN AMERICA
ISBN for complete set 0-405-02430-4

Manufactured in the United States of America

JS
345
1881
S522

Solid for Mulhooly.

109130

WHAT THE PRESS SAYS OF
SOLID FOR MULHOOLY.

"What Mrs. Stowe's '*Uncle Tom's Cabin*' was to slavery, and what Judge Tourgee's '*Fool's Errand*' is to Southern reconstruction Mr. Shapley's '*Solid for Mulhooly*' is to municipal misrule. It is the keenest and most polished satire of the age. . . . It will be the most successful gospel of municipal reform that has yet confronted our ring-ridden municipalities."—*Philadelphia Times.*

"Those who hold aloof from City politics, indifferent or ignorant about them or their workings, would do well to read this book. The inclination will then be less to laugh over some of its pages than to bring the blush of shame to an honest man's cheeks. . . . Of innumerable volumes of this character, '*Solid for Mulhooly*' is undoubtedly the best."—*New York Times.*

"One of the brightest satires ever written."—*Louisville Courier-Journal.*

"Extracts would hardly do it justice. It should be perused in its entirety. All is given with an effectiveness that cannot easily be over-praised. . . . It is the production of a writer of no common power. He has mastered completely his subject, and has seen to the bottom of it. His satire is a truly vivid picture of one of the most threatening abuses of the times."—*Boston Gazette.*

"The satire is so entirely true to the life, and written with such pungent wit, as to make its way at once to popular appreciation. . . . 'Mike Mulhooly' and 'Blossom Brick' have become as familiar as household words all over the country."—*Baltimore Gazette.*

"If anything could be a satire on American politics, it would be such a book as '*Solid for Mulhooly*,' but unfortunately for our would-be Swifts and Thackerays, our politics are so scandalous in themselves that it is impossible to satirize them. We have all met the hero of this brochure—Michael Mulhooly."—*N. Y. Evening Mail.*

"That wonderfully clever satire on City politics, '*Solid for Mulhooly*' . . . This neatest of all modern political satires . . . shows to a dot and with exquisite irony how the Bosses keep up their rule."—*Phila. Public Ledger.*

"In the municipal canvass through which we have just passed it was the quiver from which almost every arrow was drawn. It illuminated the speeches on the stump; pointed hundreds of paragraphs in the newspapers; gave spice to advertisements; flamed out on the walls; shone on the banners; became the ingenious device under which the Academy of Music was secured for a political meeting; furnished the watch-words and prototypes of the canvass; and coined a new vocabulary which at once passed current in the whole speech

WHAT THE PRESS SAYS.

of the people. It pictured the reality so vividly and reflected the popular sense so powerfully that it immediately became the life of the Campaign. As a political satire it takes very high rank. It combines the merits of polished style, caustic wit, skilful construction and trenchant truth. The chapter of maxims laid down by Blossom Brick is a masterpiece of its kind. Mr. Shapley's mastery of municipal politics, his pungent pen and his right impulses have produced what will everywhere be the flashing blade of reform."—*The Philadelphia Press.*

"It carries the American political system into the dissecting room, and pitilessly exposes the hidden seat of the disease. . . . Its interest is so great, and the conclusions which seem naturally to follow its story pierce the soul and marrow of modern English politics with so true and acute a rapier-point, that representative Radicals like Mr. Chamberlain, or disguised Radicals, as is Lord Randolph Churchill, might well republish the work for gratuitous distribution in the still unenlightened and unregenerate constituencies."—*Fortnightly Review,* "In Philistia," by Sir Lepel Henry Griffin.

"It is certain to attract as much attention in all the misruled cities of the Union as did Judge Tourgee's 'Fool's Errand' in national politics. . . . It is one of the most searching satires on municipal boss rule that has ever been given to the public."—*San Francisco Golden Era.*

"One of the most entertaining books of the day. . . . Every man acquainted with municipal politics in New Orleans may find a graphic picture in this volume of some influential emanation of the gutters or cheap grog-shop, who has become, through machine methods, the agency of rings and bosses, both rich in pocket and influential in public affairs."—*New Orleans States.*

"Paints to the life the workings of the municipal boss system that has worked great evil in cities like New York, Philadelphia, Boston, Baltimore, Cincinnati and Chicago."—*Providence Journal.*

"The graphic pictures it draws find their counterpart in every other city where machine methods dominate. Its author is evidently familiar with the whole 'boss' system in all of its phases."—*Albany Evening Journal.*

"Very bright and witty, full of sharp thrusts at the illiterate rogues who run the machine, and, as a political satire, has seldom had an equal."—*Washington Herald.*

"One of the brightest satires of the day. It hits off in excellent style the political methods in vogue in large cities."—*Boston Post.*

"A satirical, graphic, and very amusing account of the general corruption and debasement to which the Caucus system and the Irish vote have reduced American politics is given in the true story, 'Solid for Mulhooly' which we begin in this week's *England*."—*England.*

HIS PORTRAIT.
(Frontispiece.)

Copyrighted, 1889, by Gebbie & Co.

Solid for Mulhooly

A Political Satire

BY

RUFUS E. SHAPLEY

"Cats that go ratting don't wear gloves"
—Spanish Proverb

NEW EDITION

WITH ORIGINAL ILLUSTRATIONS

BY

THOMAS NAST

PHILADELPHIA
GEBBIE & CO., PUBLISHERS
1889

Copyrighted, 1889, by GEBBIE & Co.

PREFACE.

THIS sketch of "Boss-rule" was first published in 1881, at a time when the respectable people of New York, Philadelphia and other large cities were engaged in one of their periodical struggles to throw off the yoke of their local political masters, and were, for once, making an honest and serious effort at self-government by trying to select their own municipal officers. It seems hardly necessary to say that it was not especially aimed at any particular city, but was an attempt to give a picture of "the Machine" calculated to help those who denounce "Boss-rule," but assist in perpetuating it, to a better understanding of what "the Machine" is, how it is built up, and how its power is exercised and maintained—wherever "the Machine" exists.

As it has been out of print for several years (owing mainly to a desire to correct some errors in the first editions), and as constant demands are made for copies which cannot be supplied—notwithstanding the fact that it has been widely circulated by republication in the columns of newspapers in this country and in England—a new and revised edition seems to be needed.

If any one can be found innocent enough to suppose that because the people, here and there, have succeeded in temporarily overthrowing a "Boss" or set of "Bosses," Mulhoolyism has become a thing of the past—at least in *his* city—let him take off his party spectacles for a moment and study the political conditions right around him, through the medium of his local newspapers; and then, when his eyes have been somewhat opened to the truth, if they should by chance rest upon these pages, he may possibly find a meaning between the lines, and may be led to suspect that they were not written merely for yesterday or to-day.

If some one were to collate and publish each year a volume composed of cuttings from reliable newspapers throughout the country, properly classified, and showing to what extent local misgovernment actually exists in every large city, notwithstanding all previous efforts in the direction of Reform, the result would be found to be startling. A single newspaper cutting of this character is printed in the Appendix, as an illustration of Mulhoolyism in one of its most common forms to-day.

The problem of securing good government in large cities under a form of government like ours, where a newly-naturalized foreigner, possibly unable to read or speak our language, and without a dollar of taxable property in the world, has, not only a voice and a vote, but—what is still more important—a voice and vote *equal* to that of the President or Chief Justice of the United States in passing on all governmental issues, and quite as potential as that of an Astor or a Vanderbilt in all municipal matters involving the taking, through taxation, of the property of our Astors and Vanderbilts, and the expenditure of the proceeds ; where undiscriminating, unintelligent and irresponsible voters outnumber, by five to one, those who give half as much thought and care to the choice of public officials as they give to the selection of the clerks in their stores, counting-rooms and banks ; where boodle-Aldermen are consequently the rule, rather than the exception —is one that is not likely to be solved by this generation.

And intimately connected with it, because it lies at the very foundation of popular government, and not less difficult of solution, is the problem of securing the purity of the ballot-box, and preventing the election frauds which are now notoriously perpetrated, or attempted, to a greater or less extent, at every election in almost every election district in the land ; which, in the Presidential elections of 1876 and 1884, so nearly precipitated the country into open revolution, and which, unless made impossible, may, at any time in the near future, produce results so disastrous that one does not care to contemplate them.

These two vast problems *must* be solved—not theoretically, but practically—before we can surely say that our American experiment at self-government is not a failure.

The very first step, however, towards their solution is to compel the people generally to understand exactly how and why these evils are made *possible*, so that, understanding the cause, they may be willing to assist in securing such amendmendents to our State and Federal Constitutions as may be found necessary in order to provide the remedy.

Every effort towards that end, however humble or imperfect it may be, is a step in the right direction, and that is all that the author can say in defense of this sketch of "Ring-rule."

  PHILADELPHIA,
   December 25, 1888.

CONTENTS.

CHAPTER		PAGE
I.	Michael Mulhooly—His Antecedents	15
II.	His First School	19
III.	Learns the A B C of Politics	24
IV.	Studies the $x\,y\,z$ of Politics	29
V.	An Upward Leap	34
VI.	A Modern Statesman	41
VII.	A Digression	49
VIII.	A Political Gamaliel	54
IX.	The Machine	61
X.	Mulhooly Thinks of Himself	71
XI.	The Boss	76
XII.	Mulhooly Feeds with the Gods	81
XIII.	One of the City Fathers	86
XIV.	A Great Public Danger	97

CONTENTS.

CHAPTER		PAGE
XV.	The Canvass	107
XVI.	The Convention	117
XVII.	The Voice of the Press	133
XVIII.	Trouble	140
XIX.	Justice	145
XX.	A Judge Challenged	168
XXI.	One Way to Run a Campaign	172
XXII.	Another Way to Run a Campaign	183
XXIII.	The Result	198

APPENDIX—Daddy Rat as Jail-keeper 204

LIST OF ILLUSTRATIONS.

	PAGE
HIS PORTRAIT . . . . *Frontispiece*	
HIS BIRTHPLACE	16
HIS FIRST SCHOOL	20
THE BALLOT BOX— 'One election officer well in hand is worth a score of voters on the half-shell"	57
THE GREAT SUPREME	70
THE KICKER'S FATE	104
INGRATITUDE	139
POLITICAL TWINS— "And the Judge came down and shook hands with Michael Mulhooly"	166
THE GENIUS OF THE RING— "The Boss's 'I Will' is the Leaders' 'We Must'"	185
PRACTICE *vs.* THEORY	203

Solid For Mulhooly.

I.

Michael Mulhooly—His Antecedents.

MICHAEL MULHOOLY owed nothing of his greatness to high birth or early advantages. On the contrary, when he first opened his eyes his surroundings must have struck his infant mind as offering far from encouraging prospects to one about to begin life.

The ancestral halls of the Mulhoolys, situated among the bogs of County Tyrone, Ireland, consisted of a cabin of the style of architecture then fashionable in that section of the country, containing a single apartment, inhabited, at the moment of his birth, by his parents, ten rapidly-maturing pledges of their love, and two pigs, which, encouraged by the example of the elder Mulhoolys, annually contributed somewhat more than their share towards the common wealth. These humble but faithful dependents of the family joined their voices to the general welcome which greeted the arrival of the future statesman, and, as soon as he was able to crawl upon the cabin floor, they treated him as foster-brother to their own latest addition to the family circle. Thus his infancy, like that of so many of his countrymen who have become leaders of men in our own free and happy country, was spent in a condition of poverty and squalor not apparently conducive to exceptional mental growth, but which is, nevertheless, as experience has demonstrated, especially calculated to develop a genius for leadership in American politics.

Education, such as is derived from books, he did not acquire as he advanced towards the years of manhood, on account of circumstances over which he had no control. The

HIS BIRTHPLACE.—p. 16.

Copyrighted, 1889, by Gebbie & Co.

fact is, there was not a school-house, or a school-teacher, and probably not a printed book of any kind, within fifty miles of his parental home. The Mulhoolys had not learned to regard it as a disgrace that no member of the family of their acquaintance had ever learned to read and write. Had such a view of the case been suggested to them, they would, doubtless, have pointed proudly to that long line of Irish kings, from whom they, and all of their countrymen, are descended, not one of whom had ever troubled himself to acquire such useless accomplishments.

When Michael was eighteen years of age, chance brought about a change in his life which laid the foundation of his fortunes, and proved to be the starting-point in his career of greatness. Dennis Mulhooly, a distant cousin, while on a visit to the tombs of his ancestors, conceived the idea of taking the boy back with him to America, and putting him at work in his saloon, known as the "Tenth District House, by Mr. Dennis Mulhooly." So Michael, not unwillingly, yet not without many tears, bade farewell to that beautiful green isle which—as all his countrymen from time immemorial have sworn, and until time shall be no more will continue to swear—is the finest spot of green earth on this large globe; but which, nevertheless, so many of them leave at the first opportunity, and to which so few of them ever return in the flesh—owing probably to the surprising dearth of native talent for statesmanship which they discover here as soon as they land upon our hospitable shores.

II.

His First School.

UPON his arrival Michael Mulhooly began at the very foot of the ladder. The "Tenth District House, by Mr. Dennis Mulhooly," was not situated in what certain people would call a fashionable neighborhood, nor was it patronized by the most exclusive circles of society. Ministers of the gospel, bank presidents, and merchant princes never crossed its threshold. Public banquets to foreign potentates, men of letters and great generals, were never given in this hostelry. There were safer places in the world for a man to fall asleep in, if he wished to retain his watch or pocket-book.

An oyster counter, a bar, three or four chairs, and a stove, comprised all the furniture of the one low room where Mr. Dennis

Mulhooly catered to the appetites of the public. Two men were all the assistants he had required prior to the arrival of Michael, who was immediately installed in the responsible but unremunerative post of boy-of-all-work. He scrubbed the floor, carried out oyster-shells, made fires, ran errands, and occasionally lent a hand behind the oyster-counter and the bar. But he was happy. For the first time in his life he knew the luxury of having enough to eat, a warm place in which to sleep when it was cold, and clothing enough to cover his entire body. He received no wages beyond his board and clothing, but an occasional dime, earned by some menial service cheerfully performed, lit up his dreams with the rose tints of approaching prosperity and made him smile in his sleep.

But this humble bar-room, or low groggery, if you please, was the school-room in which his first lessons of life were learned, and where was revealed to his young ambition the shining ladder, like that which Jacob saw in a dream, leading up to the political Olympus upon which he was destined one day to stand and talk with the gods.

HIS FIRST SCHOOL.—p. 20.

Copyrighted, 1889, by Gebbie & Co.

Here the party-workers of the district were wont to congregate to discuss the affairs of the nation; and here, prior to party conventions, occasionally came the leaders of the ward, and, sometimes, those greater statesmen whose comprehensive minds ward-limits could not confine, to make those preliminary political arrangements for the good of the country, which they call "getting in their work."

Why continue to talk of the free-school on the hillside as the hope of the Republic, when every day, under your very eyes, you see the indubitable proof that the despised grog-shop is the true birthplace of statesmanship, and the maligned gin-mill the very cradle in which shall be rocked into manhood the coming American politician?

It was not surprising that the visits of these great men gave to the young Irish lad glimpses of a world which seemed very far above him, and in which he hardly yet dared to hope some day to live and move. It was not surprising that the fluency of their conversation about politics, sporting matters, and the women of their acquaintance; the richness and elegance of their clothing, the massiveness of their watch-chains, the size of their seal rings, the brilliancy of their diamonds, their lavish expenditure of money, and the lordly grace with which they smoked the fragrant "Reina Victoria," and ordered Pat, the barkeeper, to "set 'em up agin," or "open another bot.," dazzled his young imagination and fired his soul with the daring ambition to be, some day, so great a man and so polished a gentleman.

As he approached the age of manhood, his eyes were opened to his want of education and the advantages which he might derive from being able to read and write. Nothing daunted by the difficulties before him, he set to work in his leisure moments, under Pat's instructions, to master these accomplishments. It was slow work for such a pupil, under such a tutor, but other men have become senators, judges of the Supreme Court, aye, and even Presidents, who began to study under scarcely more favorable circumstances. Michael had industry, perseverance and ambition, and, though great was his labor, great also was his reward. When he became able to spell out, in the *Police Record*, or the *Sporting Man's Own*, the chaste and graphic accounts of the latest prize-fight, he felt something of that mental exaltation with which more fortunate school-boys read of the days and deeds of chivalry, when kings and princes contended in knightly tourney. And, as he read of these exhibitions of science and courage, he longed to be some day spoken of as a Heenan, a Morrissey, a Mace, or a Sayers.

He lost no opportunity to perfect himself in the manly art, and, as opportunities for practice were not wanting in his neighborhood, before he had reached the age of manhood he had won the reputation of being the hardest hitter and most scientific sparrer in that end of the ward.

Happy the youth who wisely selects his ideal of true manhood, and molds his own life in strict accordance with its bright example!

III.

Learns the A B C of Politics.

BEFORE he came of age he had commended himself to the party-workers who frequented the saloon by acting at the polls as the representative of a gentlemanly young clerk, who, when he offered to vote in person, was surprised at being told that he had already voted at an hour when he could have sworn he was perfecting his toilet, and who, after being rudely hustled from the polls, was glad enough to escape being beaten and afterwards arrested on the charge of attempting to violate the sanctity of the ballot.

At the age of twenty-one Michael Mulhooly was duly naturalized.

It was true that, by the ordinary methods of computing time, he supposed he had only spent two years in this country; but as the records of the court showed that two highly respectable citizens, known to and approved by the court, had made solemn oath that they had personally known the applicant for upwards of five years, during which time he had actually resided in this country, and that he was well disposed to the Government and familiar with its Constitution, it was evident that the stringent naturalization laws of the United States had not been abused.

He was now clothed in the full panoply of American citizenship. The political

> "world was all before him where to choose,
> And Providence his guide."

There was no office of election or appointment, from constable to United States Senator, to which he might not lawfully and hopefully aspire. His brand-new certificate of citizenship was far from a disadvantage to him. Judging from the experience of so many of his countrymen, it was rather a passport to place and a title-deed to a reversionary interest in the offices which they were holding, as soon as he could dispossess them. Only the office of President of the United States was hopelessly beyond his reach; or, not hopelessly, if the rapidly increasing foreign-born population of this country shall determine to erase from the Constitution of their adopted country that invidious discrimination in favor of native-born citizens which defaces it.

It is scarcely necessary to record the fact that Michael Mulhooly did not neglect to vote at the election immediately following his naturalization. Indeed, from his own statements, made that night while celebrating his political second birth, so great was his fear that his vote might not be properly counted in his own Election District, that he took the precaution to deposit another constitutional expression of his will in an adjoining District; and, to still further protect his newly-acquired rights of citizenship, he repeated this precaution against fraud in two other Districts more remote from his home. The wisdom of this course was highly commended by all his hearers; and some of them, with prophetic eye, even looked forward to the time when the country would be proud of its newly-adopted child.

Owing to a misfortune which befell Pat about this time, resulting in his temporary withdrawal from the active labors of life, by reason of his mistaking the ownership of a watch, which he said had been dropped upon the floor by a belated individual who had lost his bearings and wandered into the saloon very late one night—Michael was promoted to the post of regular bar-keeper, with a salary nominally fixed, but virtually to be determined by himself.

This promotion enlarged his opportunities for prosecuting his political studies. It placed him at once upon terms of easy familiarity with the statesmen of his acquaintance who dropped in, after a night spent in emulating the moral practices of the Roman emperors, for that inspiring morning drink which Anacreon named a "cock-tail," but which Catullus always insisted, down to the day of his death, should be called "an eye-opener." Besides, it initiated him into that mystic brotherhood—that ancient, honorable and well-dressed order founded ages ago by one Ganymede—which has, in every age, exercised such a mysterious and powerful influence over its politicians and legislators. No wonder that the poet said, "Let me mix a nation's cock-tails and I care not who makes its laws."

IV.

Studies the x y z of Politics.

AT the next election he took another forward step in his political studies.

Six brand-new American citizens from a neighboring city were so anxious to prove their gratitude to the Government for adopting them, and so determined to put down its enemies, that, dropping all business at home, they hurried over to this city and placed their services at the disposal of the Hon. Hugh McCann, a member of the State Legislature, to whom the City Committee had given $1,000 to place where it would do the most good. These public-spirited men were provided with lodgings over the "Tenth District House by Mr. Dennis Mulhooly," and to Michael was intrusted the delicate duty of guiding them to the Election Districts in which the committee had decided they could best serve their country.

One of these gentlemen had the misfortune to resemble a well-known kleptomaniac whom the police authorities of his own city were anxious to persuade to return to the sumptuous apartments which they had provided for him in the hope of curing his malady by keeping him from temptation. This resemblance struck an overly zealous police officer near the polls so forcibly, that he insisted upon taking the would-be voter, along with Michael, to the nearest station-house for identification. To this unconstitutional interference with a voter while in the exercise of the elective franchise Michael strongly objected, and commenced to discuss the constitutional questions involved with so much spirit and force that the officer, overcome by his arguments, twice lay down upon the pavement, while Michael persisted in his effort to impress upon him the soundness of his own views of the case. While thus occupied a squad of policemen under the command of a sergeant came up, and mistaking the meaning of Michael's gestures, captured him, and, not without some difficulty, at last got him inside the station-house, where they preferred against him charges of "assault and battery," "resisting an officer," and "vouching for a repeater" known to them as "Big Pat."

Michael's detention, however, lasted for only a few minutes, for Hon. Hugh McCann, who had heard of the misunderstanding, came to hunt him up, entered bail for his appearance, and assured him that early in the morning he would himself see the Boss, who would see Judge Coke and have the whole thing "squared." Michael had not yet reached that clause in the Constitution which referred to the office of Boss, and, therefore, he failed to understand, as clearly as he would have done a few years later, the nature of this office and the process of getting such matters "squared."

He had now won his political spurs. He had proved himself worthy of citizenship. He had given unmistakable evidences of possessing talents with which, by proper training, he could not fail to make his mark upon the political history of his country. He had voted once before he was of age; had voted four times at the election immediately succeeding his naturalization; at the following election had led to the polls six citizens whose votes it was known would be challenged, and had succeeded in persuading the election officers to receive five of them; had twice knocked down a police officer who interfered with him while he was discharging this delicate and important public duty, and was already under indictment for an alleged violation of the election laws, as well as for an alleged assault upon an officer of the law.

Such talents are well known to be more useful in politics than a knowledge of Greek prosody, or familiarity with the writings of Adam Smith. Such men never fail to receive that recognition from the party leaders to which such invaluable party services entitle them, and, accordingly, Michael Mulhooly was immediately placed upon his Ward Committee, and, at the next election, was duly appointed by the court an election officer to fill a vacancy, at the instance of one of the ward leaders who was a candidate for constable. This duty he also discharged so successfully that when the returns were made up by the election officers, it was found that his candidate for constable had received nearly a hundred more votes than those who kept the lists could account for, or believed had been cast.

Thus he commenced to comprehend those *unknown quantities* in politics which so materially affect results.

V.

An Upward Leap.

ABOUT this time Michael Mulhooly formed an acquaintance by which he was enabled, at a single jump, to mount several rounds of the political ladder which, in his young dreams, he had seen leading from obscurity to that Olympus above the clouds where the political gods sit and control the destinies of men.

This acquaintance he owed partly to his personal charms, partly to his recognized position among the party leaders of his ward, and partly to his fame as an athlete who could hit straight from the shoulder, and who was always ready to enter the lists and contend with the officers of the law. He had by this time learned how to improve his natural personal advantages by those arts of dress which gentlemen of his class so well understand. As he sauntered along the fashionable thoroughfares on Saturday afternoons when he was off duty, clad in light plaid breeches, tight at the knee and thence curving gracefully until nearly the whole foot was hidden, cut-away coat of darker plaid pattern, trim at the waist, and with shoulders projecting like the eaves of a Swiss chalet, red silk cravat, Derby hat, yellow kid gloves, and fancy-headed cane, you knew at a glance that you beheld one of those butterflies of the sidewalk known as "mashers."

It was not strange, therefore, that all these advantages of person, position and reputation won the regard of a woman some years his senior, whose house, situated within a square of his saloon, was frequented by most of the political leaders of his acquaintance. Nor was it strange that, flattered by her unconcealed preference, he became a constant visitor at her house, her escort to the fashionable minstrel halls and variety shows which she loved to frequent, and stood ready at all times, like a knight of old, to throw down the gage of battle to any who dared dispute her right to the title of Queen of Love and Beauty.

In her society, and that which she drew around her, his manners rapidly acquired much of that polish which he had formerly so much admired in his exemplars, and which afterwards contributed so largely to his own popularity and success in life.

In return for the many delicate services which she received from him she gave him a plentiful supply of pocket-money, many articles of jewelry indispensable to a gentleman in his station, a diamond shirt-stud, and, when Dennis concluded to purchase a larger saloon in another portion of the city, the necessary capital to buy out the old saloon, repaint, and refit it, and commence business for himself.

That was a proud night for Michael when, standing for the first time in front of his own bar, while the radiance of his diamond almost blinded his new barkeeper, he invited up a number of his political friends who had assembled to offer him their congratulations, and himself gave the order he had so often obeyed, to " set 'em up all round."

O Michael Mulhooly, honored representative of a wealthy and aristocratic constituency! if, dozing in thy seat in the nation's Capitol, thou didst ever cast thy mental eye back along the long line of thy many triumphs and achievements, say, was not that the supreme moment of moments, fullest of pride and gratified ambition and unutterable bliss, when thou didst utter, for the first time in thy life, that memorable order to thy trembling dependent, "Larry, set 'em up all round?"

But the most important of the many advantages which he derived from his association with that generous woman—over whose unmarked and nameless grave, alas! the winter winds now wail—was an acquaintance he formed at her house which greatly influenced his own career and materially affected the political history of his country.

Among the many men of note in local politics who delighted to spend their evenings in the gay circle which she drew around her, and who welcomed Michael into their midst and gladly accorded to him that high degree of consideration which was his due, as the recognized favorite of their hostess, was one Blossom Brick, who was a leader of leaders in municipal politics, and whose influence was recognized in state and national conventions. Over the wine-cup and out of the confidences of the midnight revel the casual acquaintance of these two men ripened into a close and intimate friendship, resulting from a similarity of tastes and pursuits. Blossom Brick was not slow to perceive that a man like Michael, broad of shoulder, muscular, fearless and always ready for a fight, could be of service to him in many ways. In the early days of their acquaintance this was proved to him in a manner which he could not soon forget. Late one night, just after they had parted at Michael's door, while Brick was waiting to hail some passing cab, a poor devil whom he had caused to be discharged from the Custom-House for voting contrary to his wishes in a ward convention, rendered desperate by the prospect of starvation for himself and his little family, and maddened by the rum which he had been drinking, suddenly sprang upon the unsuspecting leader, felled him with a powerful blow, jumped upon him, and threatened to avenge the wrongs, for which the law gave him no redress, by scattering upon the pavement the brains that toiled so ceaselessly for the public. For an instant Blossom Brick was compelled to look death squarely in the face, and, realizing his imminent danger, his cry for help rang sharply out on the stillness of the night and the lonely street. Fortunately it was heard by Michael, who sprang out just in time to save his friend from a terrible blow; and then he punished the assailant so severely with his fists and his boots that the poor devil had to be taken to a hospital, where he lay for six weeks in a fever, during which time one of his children died, and his wife, turned into the streets with her baby at her breast, was compelled to seek shelter in the almshouse to save herself and her infant from starvation.

Blossom Brick, knowing of Michael's many talents for politics, and desiring to extend his own empire over the ward in which the "Tenth District House" was situated, undertook, not unwillingly, the task of instructing him further in the mysteries of practical politics—a task for which he was pre-eminently qualified.

VI.

A Modern Statesman.

BLOSSOM BRICK had commenced life by learning a respectable trade; had married a respectable girl as poor as himself, and for nearly ten years had earned an honest living for himself and his family by hard work. He owned the small house in which he lived, having bought it out of his savings, and employed two workmen, by whose labor and his own he was able to make from $1,200 to $1,500 a year. Somehow he drifted into politics, for which he rapidly acquired a taste, and after serving as a delegate in several conventions, was himself nominated for the Municipal Legislature, and elected.

To defray his expenses he was compelled to mortgage his little house for half its value.

As the office paid not one cent in salary or fees, and as his income in the best of times was but a small one, his neighbors were surprised that he should be willing to pay so much for an honor which they were certain he could not afford to buy at any such price. They were also surprised to observe that he soon almost wholly neglected his business, and devoted, not only his days, but also his nights, to his public duties and political pursuits. But what surprised them most of all was to see that, as his business fell off, his income, in some unexplained way, was growing larger daily. The butcher, the baker and the grocer could not fail to note the fact that his bills with them were more than twice as large as they formerly had been, and that they were always promptly paid on presentation. Inside of a year the mortgage on the house was paid off, and the house itself was thoroughly repaired, repainted and refurnished. Two of the children were sent to boarding-school, and both himself and his wife dressed in a manner which indicated the possession of considerably more money than was necessary to support the family in their present style of living.

When Blossom Brick's term expired, he was re-nominated and re-elected; but owing to the liberality and popularity of his opponent, a wealthy manufacturer, it was generally understood that his campaign expenses were largely increased and that his re-election had cost him about $2,000. He still ostensibly carried on his business, and continued to employ two workmen, but he had entirely ceased to give it his personal attention, and it was very evident that he could not, from their labor, make much more than sufficed to pay his shop expenses.

Where, then, did this largely increased income come from? That was the question one neighbor would ask of another, when talking, as neighbors will talk, of the affairs of their more fortunate neighbor. But while they continued to talk and to wonder he continued on in his strangely prosperous career and grew richer every year. At first he bought a house adjoining his own; then a vacant lot on the other side of his house;

then two houses on the opposite side of the street, and before the close of his third term he was known to own twelve houses in the ward which he represented.

He was re-elected again and again almost without opposition, so completely had he got the working politicians of the ward, who busy themselves at delegate elections and go to conventions, under his control.

His constituents could not fail to see, however unobservant they were, that he was now a man of considerable wealth. He wore a diamond stud worth at least $1,000; he drove a pair of fast horses every fine afternoon to the park, and bought wine with the liberality of a coal-oil prince; his wife dressed in silks and velvets, and his contributions to various political organizations, independent of his expenses when a candidate for re-election, amounted to fully twice as much as he could possibly have made out of his business when he worked at it from morning till night. But he seldom even looked into the shop now, although the sign still remained up and the two workmen continued to come and go, and to talk of the business as though it was their own.

Those of his constituents who examined his record could not fail to observe some things in it worthy of attention. They saw that whenever a bill was up involving the outlay of a large sum of public money, he invariably voted in favor of the expenditure; that whenever a public improvement was proposed, he was an advocate of the improvement; that the Committee on Streets, of which he was a member, was constantly reporting bills to open, pave and grade streets, some of which no mortal eye had seen, and no mortal foot had ever trodden or would have any occasion to tread for years to come, and many of which appeared only on the city map as spaces between imaginary lines leading from No-where to No-place. They also saw that when any corporation or citizen desired legislation of pecuniary advantage, his services were, in some way, and at some time, bound to be secured, or the desired legislation failed; for Blossom Brick had become the acknowledged leader of the Municipal Legislature.

He soon came to look upon his ward as a property which he owned, or as an empire which he had the right to rule as with a rod of iron. No man in it could hope for any appointment except through him, and no man in it dared be a candidate even for school director without his permission. He even came to look upon the whole city as, in a large measure, his own private property. He made daily visits to each department of the city government and demanded appointments for his followers and the removal of those who disobeyed him, as though the departments had been created for his exclusive benefit.

He lived but for the public. In order that the people might make no mistakes he dictated what nominations should, or should not, be made. To save the people trouble, he selected in advance their candidates for legislators, for congressmen, for judges. He did not hesitate to direct legislators, congressmen and judges how they should discharge their public duties. His devotion to his party knew no bounds. At every important election he organized a campaign club which bore his name, and paraded a thousand uniformed men, bearing torches, and marching with the precision of veterans. When his form was seen advancing at the head of this formidable column, briefless young barristers on the sidewalks, filled with vague yearnings for political fame, knelt in spirit before his power, and well-fed millionaires, standing at the windows of their club-house, nodded approvingly to each other and said, "There goes a man whom the country could not afford to lose."

Such devotion to the public deserved the gratitude of the public, and that gratitude was displayed in asking him no questions as to where his money came from, or how he could grow rich by serving them without any salary. Nor was he insensible of the debt of gratitude which the people owed him, and, in order to place them under still heavier obligations, he did not hesitate to extend his empire over three other wards as large as his own.

He thus, naturally, came in time to speak of himself and his political associates as "We, the people."

VII.

A Digression.

WHEN one man owns and dominates four wards or counties he becomes a Leader. Half a dozen such Leaders combined constitute what is called a Ring. When one Leader is powerful enough to bring three or four such Leaders under his yoke he becomes a Boss, and a Boss wields a power almost as absolute, while it lasts, as that of the Czar of Russia or the King of Zululand.

The Leaders, the Ring and the Boss combined, constitute the modern system of American politics which has been found to work so successfully in all large cities, especially in those which are fortunate enough to have secured a working majority of Leaders from Ireland. It has also been tried with encouraging results in several of the oldest and largest States of the Union; and even with all the disadvantages of American birth and prejudices, some statesmen of commanding genius have been found who could thus rule their own States absolutely, for many years, by combining in themselves at once, all the functions of the Leaders, the Ring and the Boss.

The great merit of this system is that it takes from the people all the trouble of self-government and imposes that burden upon the Leaders, the Ring and the Boss, compelling them to assume all the worriment of selecting proper public servants and all the responsibility of managing public affairs, while it preserves, in unimpaired purity, the *form* of a " government of the people, by the people, and for the people."

It is true that there are still to be found in this country some very honest people, who are so slow to learn, that they cry out against this modern labor-saving system, and prefer the primitive methods of their grandfathers, who, for want of something better to do, were willing to select their own school directors, constables, judges, legislators, governors and

Presidents, notwithstanding the anxiety and labor which it involved, as well as the risk of their making unwise selections.

It is also true that there are many disappointed office-seekers whom the Leaders, the Ring and the Boss have, in their combined wisdom, found unfitted for the public service, who go about declaiming against what they call Ring-rule and Boss-rule, and magnifying what they pretend are the evil results of the operation of this beneficent system. The impartial historian of our times, while appreciating their real motives, will doubtless give them a patient hearing, and for the instruction of posterity will set down at some length their objections, and the arguments adduced in support of them.

In this sketch of a distinguished representative of this system it will be sufficient to give the following specimens of these objections to show what obstacles the Leaders, the Ring and the Boss have to overcome in their unselfish efforts to serve an ungrateful people.

These malcontents say:

"Such devotion to the public service, if exercised only for the benefit of the public, would be sublime in its unselfishness. But it would still be a despotism, pure and simple. That it is exerted, not for the good of the people, but for the exclusive benefit of the Leaders and Bosses themselves, is self-evident."

"It does not require an inspiration of genius to perceive that when a man makes from twenty to a hundred thousand dollars a year out of an office that pays no salary and does not allow car-fare or postage stamps as perquisites, he makes it *aliunde*."

"It does not require a revelation from Heaven to demonstrate that such a mathematical miracle can be performed only by Theft, for official corruption is Theft, pure and simple."

"A man would not be entitled to letters patent of the United States for the discovery that when a million of dollars is squandered in contracts controlled by three or four Leaders, who grow mysteriously rich during the transaction, they have stolen at least a portion of that money, no matter how loudly they pray in church, or how much honesty and patriotism they profess in public."

"When a common day-laborer, in twenty years devoted exclusively to politics, becomes, not only a Boss, but also a millionaire, it is perfectly safe to conclude that he is a Thief, although the statute of limitations may save him from the penitentiary."

VIII.

A Political Gamaliel.

AN astute and experienced politician once gave an applicant for a responsible and lucrative office a letter which secured his appointment and was thus laconically worded:

"*Dear Tit:*
"*The bearer understands Addition Division and Silence. Appoint him!*
"*Yours,*
"*Bill.*"

The writer of that letter was more than an epigrammatist; he was a philosopher who had sounded the profoundest depths of politics and who deserves immortality. *Addition! Division! Silence!* In those three words are contained all the wisdom of modern politics.

Blossom Brick understood every possible meaning and combination of those words. He had never read a book on political economy, but he had studied the people. For twenty years he had lived upon them and grown rich from offices that paid him not a cent in salary or fees. He knew nothing of logical forms or methods, but he knew the tree by its fruits. From political results his mind jumped to political axioms. His conversation became epigrammatic. It was not scholarly, or elegant, or refined; but it was forcible, frank, easily understood, and full of worldly wisdom. It contained the germs of a system of political philosophy not recorded in books. Like a female savage who knows nothing of the modesty of clothing, he spoke without shame of the things which he did without blushing.

Michael Mulhooly, so to speak, sat at the feet of this modern political Gamaliel, and learned wisdom. He treasured up his sayings as the words of Socrates and Plato were treasured up and transmitted to posterity by their disciples. Some of these sayings are worthy of being recorded. Here are a few specimens:

In speaking of the people and the little share they actually have in governing themselves, through popular elections, he said:

"*In politics the people are blind asses who think they can see through brick walls; they are only dangerous when they kick.*"

"*They are all right. Only make them believe they rule and they are happy.*"

"*The government means, not those who vote, but those who receive, count and return the votes.*"

"*Elections are ratification meetings which We hold to indorse our nominations.*"

"*Election laws are marked cards with which We cheat the opposition.*"

"*A man's right to vote depends upon what heading the judge sees on his ticket.*"

THE BALLOT BOX.

"One election officer well in hand is worth a score of voters on the half-shell."—p. 57.

Copyrighted, 1889, by Gebbie & Co.

A POLITICAL GAMALIEL. 57

"*It matters less how many votes you have than how many you poll ; it matters less how many you poll than how many you get counted.*"

"*One election officer well in hand is worth a score of voters on the half shell.*"

"*The result of an election is only a question of figures. A stroke of the pen before the figures 99 is as good as the votes of a hundred millionaire taxpayers—if you're smart enough to get away with it.*"

"*It is therefore more important for you to see the election officers than the voters of your District.*"

"*It is, after all, only a question of money. Here's a rule you can bet your bottom dollar on, and the man who invented it was smart enough at figures to make a million dollars out of politics in ten years. Divide the number of votes necessary to make your election absolutely certain by the number of Election Districts in which you have or can make the election officers solid, and then you know just what work you must get in in each District. Then multiply the number of Districts you've got to make solid by the cost per District and you know just about what the job'll cost.*"

"*What We want all the time is a solid election*

officer, a solid jury, a solid judge, and a solid governor, in case of slips, and the people may be d——d."

In speaking of the way in which nominations are made, he said:

"Party rules are the reins and party spirit the bit by which We drive the people all the time."

"A scratcher is a traitor—to Us."

"The temporary chairman is the convention. He's an 8 to 7 man all the time."

"If you can't make a nomination yourself, be sure to name your man; but be d——d sure he's honest enough—to divide."

"Put up a slate you want broken and get in your real work behind it. When the people have broken your slate with their heels they take a rest, and everything's lovely."

"The meanest thing in the world is a Ring—that counts me out."

"If you want office, young man, kneel to the Boss first, then to the Leaders, then to the people, and

afterwards to the Lord, if you have any spare time left!"

In speaking of bribery and corruption, he said:

"*A man who's d——d fool enough to call in witnesses to see him take a bribe deserves the extreme penalty of the law.*"

"*The man who gives a bribe can't tell, and the fellows who divide it wont; so the law protects the boys all the time.*"

"*Oaths of office are the most useful things I know of—they make the people believe in Us.*"

"*The man who intimates that I can be bought insults me—not the fellow who talks biz.*"

"*The larger the divisor the smaller my share; therefore I want as few in the pot as possible.*"

"*Official advertising is the Pain-Killer of Politics.*"

"*Give the people plenty of taffy and the newspapers plenty of advertising—then help yourself to anything that's lying around loose.*"

"*A chunk of meat will cure the bark and the bite of a dog; therefore if you don't know how to silence a Reformer, it's your own fault.*"

"*Honesty is the best policy by all odds—when you're in a hole.*"

"*It's cheaper to buy with promises than with cash.*"

And once, when there were signs of a rebellion against one of their candidates, he said solemnly:

"*If the people ever tumble to our game—Hell will be to pay!*"

IX.

The Machine.

UNDER the tuition of such a master, Michael Mulhooly could not fail to make rapid strides in the study of practical statesmanship.

As a member of the Ward Committee, as the proprietor of a saloon which was becoming the party head-quarters of the Ward, as well as of his Election District, and, as the intimate friend of so powerful a Leader as Blossom Brick, his influence grew so rapidly that in a short time he was chosen as the representative of his Ward in the City Committee.

From this vantage ground he could now survey the whole political field, and study the party organization in all its divisions and subdivisions. He saw that it was a political machine as complicated, as ingenious, as perfect as the works of a watch; that it had its little wheels and big wheels all moving within and upon and around each other in perfect harmony and with a common purpose; that it had its regulator, its hair-spring, its balance-wheel, and its great, strong main-spring which kept the whole in motion, in obedience to the will of the master spirit who held the key and understood its use.

He proceeded to study it, somewhat after the manner of an apprentice who undertakes to study the works which he must be able some day to make, and who, therefore, holds them up between his eye and the light and, having thus gained a comprehension of them as a whole, proceeds slowly and carefully to take them to pieces, examining each wheel and pinion so as to understand its composition, form, function and relation to every other part, and then endeavors slowly and carefully to put them together again, so that they will once more perform their perfect work.

He saw that the party organization was

composed primarily of District Committees, Ward Committees and the City Committee, and, secondarily, of Conventions to place in nomination candidates for various offices to be chosen at elections held by the people; and that all these various members or parts of the organization were provided for and governed by a system of laws called Party Rules, which operated like the Constitution and laws of a great Commonwealth.

He saw that while this perfect party organization was ostensibly created to insure the success of the party, and, thereby, the good of the people, it had been so ingeniously devised as to compel obedience on the part of the great body of voters, while it placed the entire control of the whole machinery in a central head or master-spirit, composed of one man, or two men, or half a dozen men, according to circumstances; or in other words, of the Leaders, the Ring, and the Boss.

He saw also, that however the Party Rules might be modified from time to time, in the apparent interest of the great body of voters, in their practical operation they would still be found to contribute only toward strengthening the power of those who, by the natural tendency of party organizations towards centralization of power, might, from time to time, constitute the Leaders, the Ring and the Boss.

He saw that by this system the Leaders, the Ring, and the Boss practically nominated all candidates, and as—where the party is largely in the majority, and the voters can be kept in the traces—a nomination is equivalent to an election, they, therefore, practically appointed all public officers, under the form of an election by the people.

He saw that this system necessitated a species of competitive examination, not contemplated by the advocates of Civil Service Reform, but calculated to strengthen the system and perpetuate the power of those who control it. He saw that any one desiring to enter the lists as a candidate must give satisfactory proofs that he had already rendered valuable services to Them; that no other man could fill the place with such advantage to Them; and that he would at all times, and under every circumstance, implicitly obey Their orders, irrespective of consequences, legal, moral, social, or political. He saw that if, for instance, one desired to be a candidate for judicial honors, he must be able to give undoubted assurances, either by his past record, or by some satisfactory pledges, that he would hold his office as of Their gift, and might be at all times safely and privately conferred with by Them, so as to be instructed how to administer Justice, and yet further Their interests in all matters falling within the scope of his judicial functions.

He soon saw that this whole system was founded on (*a*) the tendency of every voter to work in the traces, and vote for any man ostensibly nominated by the party; (*b*) the strict enforcement of the Party Rules; and (*c*) the judicious distribution of the 4,036 regularly salaried officers in the various departments of the city government, with a salary list of $6,595,625.50; the various municipal, State and national offices to which only perquisites and *aliunde* profits are attached; the various appointments which may be, from time to time, controlled in the various State and national offices, such as the Custom-House, Post-office, Treasury, etc., and of the various contracts for public work, involving the outlay of millions of dollars given to contractors who are willing not only to Rebate, but also to properly control at all times the thousands of workmen whom they employ in the public service.

His estimate showed that, directly and indirectly, nearly ten thousand persons were employed, and nearly $10,000,000 expended annually in the public service through these various channels.

He next endeavored to learn something about how these offices were distributed, and for that purpose he made up a list of the members of the City Committee, and the occupation of each member, with the following result, viz.:

CITY COMMITTEE.

Ward.	Member.	Occupation.	Salary.
1.	Dennis McNulty,	Department of Taxes.	$2,500.
2.	Michael McCann,	" Water.	2,000.

THE MACHINE. 67

3. Patrick McBride,	Department of Water,	$2,000.
4. Timothy McCrory,	" Streets.	1,800.
5. James McElwee,	" Fires.	2,000.
6. Owen McPeak,	" Wharves.	1,900.
7. Michael Mulhooly,		
8. James McPodd,	" Health.	2,250.
9. John McGuiggen,	" Markets.	1,800.
10. Tim. O'Hoolahan,	" Sewers.	2,000.
11. Blossom Brick,	Municipal Legislature.	?.
12. James O'Rafferthy,	Department of Parks.	2,200.
13. Michael McGaughey,	" Taxes.	2,500.
14. Thomas McNobb,	Dep't of Public Buildings.	2,350.
15. John Smith,		
16. Patrick O'Donahugh,	Department of Fires.	2,000.
17. James Kelly,	" Schools.	?.
18. Michael Mulligan,	" Streets.	2,200.
19. Bernard McGoul,	" Wharves.	1,900.
20. James McGinnis,	" Water.	2,000.
21. Robert Lannigan,	Candidate for Municipal Legislature.	

He also made up a similar list of the Presidents of the various Ward Committees, and the occupation of each, with the following results, viz.:

PRESIDENTS OF WARD COMMITTEES.

Ward. President.	Occupation.	Salary.
1. Dominick McGrody,	Department of Fires.	$1,500.
2. Daniel McMaekin,	" Wharves.	1,200.
3. Thomas McCue,	" Health.	1,400.
4. John McTee,	" Streets.	1,200.
5. Michael McLaughlin,	" Sewers.	1,000.
6. James O'Dowd,	" Taxes.	1,250.

7.	John O'Toole,	Department of Parks.	$1,000.
8.	Patrick O'Rourke,	" Water.	1,300.
9.	Bernard O'Leary,	" Markets.	1,400.
10.	Sandy McDermott,	Dep't of Public Build'n's.	1,000.
11.	Patrick Kelley,	" Justice.	1,200.
12.	Timothy McElhone,	" Police.	1,000.
13.	James O'Donnel,	" Treasury.	1,500.
14.	John McFall,	" Comptroller.	1,200.
15.	Dennis McCrystal,	" Schools.	?.
16.	John McCrossin,	" Public Build'n's.	1,200.
17.	Michael McGahey,	" Parks.	1,000.
18.	Larry McCusker,	" Water.	1,200.
19.	James McGurrity,	" Taxes.	1,500.
20.	Hugh McDaid,	Contractor on Streets.	?.
21.	John Brown, Candidate for Municipal Legislature.		

He did not attempt to make up a complete list of the five hundred and thirty members of the various Ward Committees, or of the Chairmen and members of the five hundred and thirty District Committees, or of the two secretaries of each of these City, Ward and District Committees, or of the many local Leaders, for whom there is no room on Committees, but who render valuable services in Ward, District and City Conventions, in return for the appointments which they hold.

His examination, though imperfect, had been carried far enough to show him these important results:

1. That nearly every member of the City Committee and of the various Ward Committees held a lucrative position by the appointment of some Leader whose orders he was compelled to obey.

2. That, as these Committees fix the times and places for holding Convention, select the temporary Chairman to organize them, and decide all disputes and appeals, they practically control all Conventions.

3. That every one of these four thousand and thirty-six Department employees is presumed to be able to go to a Convention when ordered to do so, or to send in his place a person who will obey orders; and that these appointees, as well as the thousands of others in other offices and employments, are so distributed through the different Wards as to be able, when acting in concert, to control a large majority of all the Wards.

4. That the Leaders had, in one way or another, obtained control of one Department of the City Government after another, until more than four-fifths of all the men employed directly and indirectly in the public service

and paid by the public money were under their immediate orders.

5. That the Leaders were themselves subject to the orders of the Boss, who had "made" most of them, and without whose favor they would be comparatively powerless.

6. *That the Boss was the Great Supreme.*

"THE GREAT SUPREME."—p. 70.

Copyrighted, 1889, by Gebbie & Co.

X.

Thinks of Himself.

MICHAEL MULHOOLY'S reflections, based on his political observations, resolved themselves into the form of elementary rules which he would probably have put into something like this shape:

1. *To succeed, you must be useful. Therefore make yourself useful at the polls. It may be done in many ways.*

2. *Attach yourself as soon as possible to a Leader. The greater his power the better; and the more useful you can be to him the greater will be your reward. Whoop for him all the time!*

3. *Secure the control of your own District at the earliest possible moment. Setting 'em up freely and frequently for the boys is the best way to begin.*

4. Then extend your influence to the adjoining District, and so on from one to another, until you can control a majority of the Districts of your Ward. To do this, you must form combinations with men like yourself, and secure employment for others in return for the services you render the Leaders.

5. When you have gained the control of your own Ward, you are yourself a Leader, and are entitled to something soft.

6. From this time forward, the more candidates you help to nominate and the more men you get appointed by them, the higher your rank among Leaders and the more abundant your harvest.

7. Always remember that in politics the Boss is God!

He was now in a position which he thought entitled him to some reward for his labors. He had represented his Ward in the City Committee for nearly a year; had on several occasions voted on important questions, according to Blossom Brick's wishes—the highest law that he then knew; had friends for whom he had secured employment, and who would stand by him in every Election District of the Ward, and consequently felt that, with the favor of the Boss, he could easily secure a majority of the delegates to a Ward Convention. Without that favor, he knew it would be useless for him to attempt anything.

He looked over the entire field to see what position there was within his reach which would best enable him to make money and, at the same time, to extend his political influence. He saw that if he asked for and received an appointment in one of the City Departments his salary would be limited, his perquisites small, his time n longer his own, and that he would lose his independence and make no headway towards that leadership to which he aspired. He saw that to obtain a seat in the State Legislature he would have to defeat the sitting member, who was popular with the party workers, and useful to the Leaders, whom he had faithfully served for two sessions. He saw also that, even if he could secure the nomination, his campaign expenses would more than consume his whole salary, and that an inexperienced legislator would have little opportunity to make anything *aliunde*, by reason of recent changes in the State Constitution which, to a great extent, prohibited special legislation. He fully realized that he was too young in politics to hope for any valuable city or "Row" office. But he saw from the example of his friend Blossom Brick, that if a member of the Municipal Legislature fails to make his position pay, both pecuniarily and politically, he has no one to blame but himself. He also saw that there would be a chance for him to enter this body from his Ward if he could secure the Boss's approbation.

The member at that time, J. Augustus Dootson, Esq.,—a young lawyer whose prepossessing appearance, perfect taste in pantaloons and positive genius for leading a German, had secured him a rich wife with a handsome income and a brown-stone house on a fashionable square—had been nominated by the Leaders as a means of conciliating certain wealthy tax-payers of the Ward who had been seized with the Reform-fever and had threatened to overthrow the Leaders and their system. But this young gentleman, upon taking his seat, had endeavored to walk alone, or, in the language of Blossom Brick, " to set up in business for himself," and consequently it was not probable that those whom he had thus insulted when they sought to guide his inexperienced legislative footsteps would favor his renomination.

Michael, therefore, concluded that as he might go further and do much worse, he would suggest the subject of his own candidacy for a seat in the Municipal Legislature to his friend Blossom Brick. This he did without delay and found that the idea was highly commended by that sagacious statesman. It was accordingly determined that the subject should be diplomatically opened to the Boss, and that Michael, who had never seen Him, should be presented on the first favorable opportunity. A few days later Blossom Brick called and took the young aspirant for legislative honors into the presence of the All-powerful, to learn His pleasure.

XI.

The Boss.

MICHAEL had heard so much of Him, of His power, and of His mighty wrath when offended, that his legs naturally shook when they were about to usher him, for the first time, into that august Presence. He was not quite certain that he would not find Him seated upon a throne, clad in regal purple, wearing a crown of diamonds, and surrounded by all the splendor of royalty.

When he entered the modestly furnished private office where this Great Ruler received His reports from His ten thousand faithful subjects, and issued those secret orders which were the cause of so much happiness or misery, by which men were set up or destroyed at His awful pleasure, his sense of relief was scarcely less than his feeling of disappointment to see a plainly-dressed, ordinary-looking man, reclining negligently in an arm-chair, with His feet resting on the top of a table before Him, laughing and talking, like any ordinary mortal, with two or three other plainly-dressed, ordinary-looking men, who wore their hats in His presence, and did not perceptibly tremble when they addressed Him.

The conversation related to a certain member of Congress who was seeking a renomination, and who had declared, as some one stated, that he intended to return to Congress—with the Boss's permission, or without it.

At this remark the Boss's face flushed hotly, and, turning angrily towards Blossom Brick, He said—with a slight accent that assured Michael he was about to approach a fellow-countryman: "D'ye hear that, Brick? Didn't I make him befoor, just to plaze you; and didn't I tell ye the whipper-strapper 'd be agin Us?"

"Indeed you did," replied Brick, "and now We've got to teach him a lesson. We'll show him that We make Congressmen."

Then calling up Michael, he introduced him to the Boss, who bade him "sit down," and, without changing his position, said, "Mi friend Brick tells Me you'd like to go till the Municipal Legislature from your Waard. I can tell you wan thing—I'm agin Dootson. I don't like 'im. I made 'im befoor, as me friend Brick 'll tell you, and now he's putting on airs, and I mane to punish 'im. I'd like to know where he'd have been but for Me?"

Then turning to one of the other gentlemen, he said: "D'ye know that afther all I did for that fellow Dootson, I sint for 'im whin the bill to pave Goodenough sthreet was up, and tould 'im I was much interisted in it, and that I would thank him to vote for it. And what d'ye think he answered Me? That the respictible peaple of his Waard were opposed to it, and therefore he couldn't do it. Then I tould 'im to go back to the respictible peaple of his Waard, and ask them to re-nominate 'im, but that I'd be agin 'im annyhow. And d'ye know that he hasn't spooken to Me sence? Sometimes I think I'll give up polatics intirely. The more you do for some peaple, the more ungrateful they are to ye."

The gentleman addressed laughed, and said, "Oh! you always say that."

Then the Boss, who was evidently smarting under the recollections of the ingratitude with which He was treated, put on His hat, commenced to pull on His overcoat, and Blossom Brick said, "Come, Mike, let's go!" and the interview terminated.

Michael himself had not spoken a word, and he went away entirely uncertain as to whether the Boss intended to "make 'im," or not.

But though the interview had not been all that he might have desired, it was, nevertheless, of great political significance. He had climbed to the radiant summit of the political Olympus; had stood at the very foot of the throne; had listened to the hurtling of the direful thunderbolts hurled wrathfully down towards the earth in his very presence, and had talked, face to face, with the great Jove, Himself.

XII.

Feeds with the Gods.

A FEW days later Michael Mulhooly was bidden to a banquet of the Gods. An invitation came from a gentleman whom he had never seen, but of whom he had frequently heard as a favorite contractor, who furnished half a million dollars' worth of supplies annually to the city, to an excursion and banquet given to the Boss, and such of the Superior Deities and such of His most highly-favored subjects as He might indicate it was His pleasure to have invited.

It was a banquet worthy of the Gods. Everything that could charm the eye, delight the ear, tempt the palate, please the stomach and elevate the soul was provided most bountifully. Everything was arranged so as to convey some delicately-suggested compliment to the political Father of Gods and men.

Fragrant beds of many-colored flowers arrested the eye, and showed His monogram worked in the sweetest and most beautiful rose-buds, as though nature had busied herself to do Him honor. Birds of gorgeous plumage, half hidden in ivy-covered bowers, called out His name to every passer-by, as though the pleased universe could not keep the joyful secret of His presence. The music consisted of the old songs and national melodies that He most loved to hear, and which, in His hours of relaxation, He was wont to hum softly to Himself. Wine, sweet as the honey of Hymettus, and cold as the snows that melt on the top of Mount Hybla, flowed from gigantic bottles labeled, in letters of pure gold, "The Boss"—His own favorite brand, named after Himself.

The toasts proposed were all variations of one theme—the honor due from men and Gods to Him; and the speeches all took up and repeated this refrain in all the varieties of tone and semitone, like a musical symphony.

The guests being of His own selection were worthy of His presence. With the exception of Michael Mulhooly, a Judge, a Governor, and the liberal Amphitryon of the feast, none were present except those Superior Deities who presided over Departments, or whose dominions consisted of not less than two or three Wards.

Blossom Brick, as His acknowledged favorite, sat at His right hand and whispered in His ear, from time to time, those brilliant inspirations of statesmanship that were constantly flashing like meteors across his own mighty mind.

Juno and Minerva were, of course, absent. Even lovely Venus herself had not been invited. It was not customary to bid to these stag-banquets Terpsichore or Thalia, Melpomene or Urania, or any of their talented sisters, and even Hebe was forbidden to show her pretty face and trim, lightly-clad figure on such occasions. Not that the female divinities were put wholly out of mind; for the conversation would sometimes drift from graver themes to such lighter subjects as the size of Terpsichore's ankle, or the perfect swell of Venus's matchless bust. But their conversation dwelt mainly on weightier matters, such as the political affairs of men and the destinies in store for them.

It was customary, too, on such occasions to determine who, among the sons of men, by reason of their superior fidelity, were entitled to political rewards; and who, on account of their disloyalty, were especially deserving of punishment. These were also considered fitting opportunities for the Superior Deities to ask for those political favors for their friends which, in His moments of greatest good humor, He was accustomed to distribute among them.

The hours glided imperceptibly by, and as the day began to wane, the Boss soothed and melted by the flatteries which rose around Him, looked approvingly towards Michael Mulhooly, and said once or twice with emphasis, "I'm fur 'im. Yis, I'm fur 'im," and then added angrily, " I mane to tache young Dootson what it costs to defy Me. I'll show 'im what the respictible peaple of his Waard can do for any wan that's agin Me!"

This was a decree of Fate. It affected the destiny of a great people, and materially altered a nation's history.

XIII.

One of the City Fathers.

MICHAEL MULHOOLY was duly nominated and elected to the Municipal Legislature, and thus became one of the "City Fathers."

When his campaign was over he found that it had cost him considerably more than he had expected to be called upon to pay for the honor to which he aspired, and at first he failed to see clearly how he was to get back the $1,400, which he had expended in paying his assessment, his contribution to the "Michael Mulhooly Club," in the purchase of a diamond for the Boss, and several other investments of a confidential character, which it is not necessary or proper to particularly set forth.

But before he had been in his seat many

months several opportunities occurred, of which he was not slow to take advantage, which enabled him to make up all he had spent and to lay the foundation of his fortune.

The firm of Stone, Lime & Co., of which the Amphitryon of the feast was a member, impressed with the influence which must of necessity be wielded by one whose relations with the Boss were as intimate as were Michael Mulhooly's, enlisted that rising statesman's interest in passing an ordinance which would result in their furnishing a large quantity of material for some public works, and promised, in the event of his success, to leave with him a contribution of $5,000, to be expended in any way which he might deem for the best interest of the party to which they were all so devotedly attached. Michael Mulhooly did his work so well and disposed of the fund so advantageously that over $2,500 of it remained in his hands for future distribution.

Not long afterwards the firm of Iron, Steel & Co. conceived the project of building for the city a bridge, at a cost of $1,500,000. Understanding the kind of argument which could be most successfully used to secure the passage of legislation of this character, they named a price which was $250,000 larger than the sum which would yield them a clear profit of $250,000, on the work. The project was, at first, violently opposed, and then the wisdom of their allowing themselves so large a margin became apparent. Their confidential agent sought out Blossom Brick, who was one of the strongest opponents of the measure when it was first proposed, and in the course of two or three short interviews on the street, presented the case in so new and favorable a light to that discerning statesman, that he immediately moved the appointment of a sub-committee to ascertain and report, " What would be the probable increase in the taxable value of property in twenty-five years, by reason of the proposed improvement," of which sub-committee he was appointed Chairman. Their report was so favorable and showed so clearly that in less than a hundred years the public would be so fond of this bridge that they would insist on having another one just like it, at no matter what cost, that the measure passed the House by a majority of two votes. It subsequently passed the Chamber, of which Michael Mulhooly was a member, by a still closer vote.

The firm's confidential agent subsequently reported to his employers that the whole of the $250,000 had been distributed in ways that they were not required by law to know anything about.

The private memorandum which he afterwards tore up, showed a list of initials set opposite various sums ranging from $25,000 down to $200. Upon it were these letters and figures:

"B. B. $25,000."
"M. M. 7,500."

Later in the year the M. & V. C. R. R. Company desired the privilege of laying their tracks through certain streets, and the transfer of a certain unused tract of land belonging to the city, upon which they proposed to build a freight depot. The necessary legislation was regarded by the company as of such value that the sum of $50,000 was placed in the hands of Sanderson Oily, Esq., the regular counsel for the company, to be expended by him in wine, cigars and matches for the refreshment of the members of the Committee on Streets and the Committee on Railroads while listening to his elaborate argument to prove that the more privileges a city grants to railroad companies the richer the citizens become, and that the less unimproved real estate it owns the less money must be raised by taxation to pay for the removal of the brick-bats and tomato-cans that necessarily accumulate in large quantities upon such unimproved and worse than useless property. His arguments were so unanswerable that the desired legislation was secured; but, being a lawyer, he kept no memoranda of the items in which he had expended this large sum. Blossom Brick, however, in talking over the subject with Michael Mulhooly, declared that he himself had paid out less than half the sum put up in his hands, and yet had brought over all the members he had agreed to fix, and had put away $8,000 in government bonds which "couldn't squeal." He also added that if Michael didn't know better how to measure the men he undertook to make solid he ought to go to farming, and that it was nothing but his own d——d stupidity he had to blame for having only $2,500 left for himself.

Of course, as soon as Michael Mulhooly had fairly entered upon his duties as a legislator he commenced to speculate in stocks of all kinds and especially in Street Passenger Railway Stocks—the favorite investment of legislators—and made daily visits to the office of his brokers.

When one is a legislator one is constantly liable to suspicion and frequently in danger of investigating committees. There are people who are ready to swear that a legislator is a bribe-taker as soon as he shows symptoms of the too-common complaint of growing rich without work. There are people who can not be made to understand how the business of a bar-room that never could be made to pay $1,500 a year can be made to yield an annual income of $15,000, or more, as soon as its proprietor becomes a member of the Municipal Legislature; or how a lawyer, whose practice never before would pay his office-rent, can, by wholly neglecting his office to attend to the daily and nightly meetings of his Committees, live like a prince and buy wine like a Russian Grand Duke. Nevertheless, such apparent miracles are of by no means rare occurrence. Therefore, when one is thus liable to be misjudged, it is a great satisfaction to be able to refer to that lucky rise in P. T. & X., which netted nearly $10,000 clear, and to hint at the probability of realizing, inside of six months, a quarter of a million out of the Bully-Boy-Put-Your-Money-Down-Here Mine. Of course, the mine is too far away—and too deep—to be investigated; and no respectable broker will open his books and exhibit a customer's account to any impertinent newspaper reporter.

But, however it happened, as the years went on Michael Mulhooly grew fat in body and pocket. After entering upon his second term he sold out the saloon, bought real estate, and told the canvasser for the City Directory that his occupation was "Gentleman." Under the generous living in which he indulged, and the summer-like calm of the soul begot of a still and quiet conscience, he gradually developed that rotundity of person which is almost invariably found to accompany and indicate a genius for statesmanship. As he walked the streets, splendid from head to foot in shining broadcloth, white cravat, white overcoat, white hat, diamond shirt-studs, yellow kid gloves and patent-leather boots; turning the scales at 230; slick, oily, rotund and smiling; bowing to the right hand and to the left with something of the dignity of a duke and the grace of a Brummel; now stopping to press the hand of a hard-working constituent, and impress him with the honor of a great man's notice; now inviting "the boys" into a neighboring saloon, and now stopping a Judge to inquire after the health of his Honor's family, it was not strange that he seemed, both to his constituents and to himself, as one whom the people justly delighted to honor.

His political influence also grew with the expansion of his fortune, mind and body. He was now high in the rank of Leaders, and his knees no longer shook when he entered the presence of the Boss. He had served faithfully those who had "made" him, and they found no fault with him for having likewise served himself. He was the undisputed master of his own Ward. There was not an Election District whose active partymen he had not provided with places, and from which he could not, at any time, command the delegate. This was true of even the two Districts which included within their boundaries the fashionable avenues occupied mainly by bank-presidents and millionaires. It is true that his acquaintance with such men was not of a strikingly intimate character; but such men rarely go to delegate elections, and when they do, their votes count for so little that they are seldom counted at all.

Up to this time Michael Mulhooly's public

career had been like a cloudless summer day. He would probably have been satisfied to remain for some years longer in this position of honor and usefulness, had he not seen rising just above the political horizon a cloud scarcely larger than a man's hand. But he knew that it threatened a storm, and from boyhood he had been noted for that rare foresight which taught him how to seek shelter in rainy seasons. For some time what was called the "Reform movement" had been advocating the election of what was also called "a better class" of men to the Municipal Legislature. Not that this movement in the slightest degree affected the certainty of his own renomination and re-election, for his hold upon the party was too strong, and the party majority was too great, for any such movement to be able to defeat him in his Ward. But he saw that this Reform movement, by concentrating all its force upon this one point, might secure control of both branches, elect both Presidents, and thus be enabled to reconstruct all the standing Committees.

In the event of such a change occurring he foresaw the likelihood of his being removed from the Chairmanship of his Committee, to which he owed his political power and his opportunities for usefulness to himself and his friends. He therefore concluded that it was time for him to look for promotion. He had been a citizen for nearly ten years; had faithfully served his party during all that time; had by his own industry and talents become a gentleman of leisure and a taxpayer; was worth at least $100,000, and, therefore, he felt that he was entitled to enter a broader and higher field of usefulness, and he determined to be a candidate in his District for a seat in the Congress of the United States.

XIV.

A Great Public Danger.

THE Congressional District in which Michael Mulhooly lived was composed of five Wards. It had been represented for one term by Charles Chauncey Chumbleson, Esq., a gentleman of large wealth and aristocratic lineage, who, knowing nothing of political methods, delegate elections and District Conventions, but desiring to hold an official position at Washington—for the sake of his two daughters, who were anxious to become, by marriage, the Marchioness of Carabas, and the Duchess of Dorking—thought the simplest and surest plan was to pay $5,000 for the honor to Tim O'Hoolahan, Barney McGhoul and Paddy O'Rourke, a Committee who agreed to place in his hands, for that sum, the certificate of his nomination by the party Convention.

This highly creditable and satisfactory arrangement was carried out to the letter by each of the contracting parties, and, as the majority in the District was nearly nine thousand, he was duly elected without further trouble and with comparatively little additional expense. He continued to contribute liberally to all the party organizations and associations in his District, but, when he had done that, he considered that he had faithfully discharged his full duty to his Constituents-by-purchase, and would not enter a department to ask for a single appointment. Nor did he feel bound to break the fashionable calm of his existence by useless efforts to make himself heard by uninterested and inattentive Members on the floor, or by the almost indiscernible spectators in the far-distant galleries.

The Hon. Charles Chauncey Chumbleson thus made two fatal mistakes. The party-workers who make nominations consider that the main object and purpose of sending a

Representative to Congress is to secure, through him, the appointment of the greatest possible number of men from his District to positions in the Navy Yard, the Post-Office, the Treasury, the Custom-House and the various Departments at Washington. On the other hand, business men and people of intelligence, who care nothing for and know nothing about these appointments and the important part they play in practical politics, believe that a Congressman should have broad, profound and decided views of his own on all questions affecting the policy of the national government at home and abroad, and that he should be able to impress those views upon his colleagues and upon the Country. It was evident, therefore, that however widely these two classes differed on this subject, they entirely agreed that Hon. Charles Chauncey Chumbleson was a failure as a member of Congress, and ought not to be renominated. He was, nevertheless, a candidate, and hoped that, through the agency of Tim O'Hoolahan, he might be again able to buy a certificate for a second term, just as he was accustomed to buy a pug dog for his daughter, or a new coupé for his wife.

The Reform element of the party, led by men of wealth, culture and character, had determined to nominate and elect Mr. Henry Armor, whom they considered in every way worthy of such a position, and who, by his eloquent speeches and scholarly articles, published in the magazines to which he was a contributor, was recognized as the leader of the Reform movement. Though still a young man, he had given unmistakable evidences of the possession of talents of the very highest order, and had already won a national reputation as an orator. He possessed all the advantages of good birth, an admirable education improved by foreign travel, large means which enabled him to practice the profession of his choice without being dependent upon it for his livelihood, an acquaintance with most of the literary men and prominent statesmen of the country, and a large circle of intimate and admiring friends, to whom his modesty, genial manners, purity of heart, manliness of character and brilliant intellect had greatly endeared him.

He was the irreconcilable enemy of the new school of politics of which Michael Mulhooly was the perfect type. He believed in the almost obsolete methods of his fathers, and contended that the people not only had the right to select their own servants for themselves, but also that they had the right to do it without the aid, instrumentality, agency or dictation of any Leader or set of Leaders. He professed to believe that the people themselves could select more honest and more capable public officers than had ever been, or ever would be, selected for them by the Leaders, the Ring and the Boss, however exceptionally qualified for the discharge of this duty many of them might be, after a few years' residence in this country, by reason of their foreign birth.

He claimed that, as the stockholders of a Bank choose their Board of Directors, and as the Directors in turn choose a President and a Cashier on account of their proved capacity and integrity, and not on account of their political views, so the Mayor, Comptroller and Treasurer of a great city should be selected, not because of their services to this party or to that, but because of their special qualifications for these offices and their approved fidelity to the people and to the high trusts reposed in them by the people. He even advocated that un-American idea known as Civil Service Reform, which teaches that the clerks and letter-carriers in the Post-Office ought not to be turned out every time a new Post-Master is appointed, and their places filled by others who, though able to go to Conventions, know nothing of the new duties required of them; and that clerks in the United States Treasury Department who have had twenty years' experience in the public service are not necessarily unfitted to remain and unworthy of trust because they do not belong to the same political party which has happened, by an 8 to 7 vote, to elect the incoming President.

He even went beyond these impracticable dreamers and taught seditious doctrines of the most dangerous character. While admit-ing that in a Republic great political parties are necessary to promote great political doctrines, he contended that the natural and inevitable tendency of every party is, in the course of time, to permit the entire control of the party to fall into the hands of some selfish man, or set of men, and thus to become corrupt and unworthy of public confidence; and that, just as destructive thunder-storms are necessary in nature to purify the atmosphere from pestilential and deadly vapors, so the occasional defeat of the party in power is essential for its own purification, in order to break off the corrupt hold of party dictators and remand back to the people the power wrested from them.

He contended that this party purification could not be effected by amendment of the party rules, or tinkering at the party machinery, because the party rules and the party machinery are, and always must be, completely under the control of these party dictators. He claimed that the hope of the country for the future was in the Independent Voter, who would antagonize his party when he found that it was becoming corrupt, and in the "Scratcher," who would not hesitate at any time to erase from his ticket the name of an improper candidate improperly placed upon it. He often said, "The Independent Voter and the Scratcher are the country's safest, cheapest and best doctors. You must starve the Boss system to death to kill it." He boldly attacked those party dictators whom he called "*our political gods of Irish parentage*," and he denounced Boss-rule as an insult to a free people, a disgrace to American civilization, and the shame of our age and country.

These dangerous views—in which he was sincere, however much mistaken—he advocated in eloquent, scholarly and plausible speeches, which attracted universal attention and made not a few converts.

It was, therefore, manifestly unsafe to permit such a man to attain any position of influence and power in his party. His success would not only greatly extend his opportunities for preaching and promulgating these seditious doctrines, but it would be at once an

THE KICKER'S FATE.—p. 104.

Copyrighted 1889, by Gebbie & Co.

insult and a menace to those who had done so much to build up the party and promote its success.

The great Leaders and the Boss held a solemn council. They felt that a grave public danger was impending over the party and the country, and They determined that his nomination must be prevented at any cost.

Just at this opportune moment Blossom Brick suggested that Michael Mulhooly, who had proved his fidelity to Them and to Their system in numberless ways, and who would have his own Ward "solid" to start with, would be the best man They could find in the Congressional District to support for this nomination. The emergency was indeed a grave one, and this suggestion at the time proved to be a masterpiece of statesmanship. They saw at once that They could fill Michael Mulhooly's place with a man of equal fidelity, and that by promoting him to Congress his influence would be extended over five Wards, and that they would thus be able to control a large number of valuable appointments which had been wholly lost to Them by the utter incapacity of Hon. Charles Chauncey Chumbleson.

The Boss, according to his custom, spoke first and spoke briefly. He said, "I'm fur 'im;" and Blossom Brick replied, "That settles the business. We're solid for Mulhooly."

It was, therefore, immediately determined that Michael Mulhooly should be the next Congressman from that Congressional District, and accordingly the decree went forth through every Department under Their control, and to the remotest corners of Their dominions.

XV.

The Canvass.

MICHAEL MULHOOLY at once set to work to canvass his Congressional District in a manner which indicated that he thoroughly understood his business.

He did not waste his time hunting up ministers of the gospel, or bank presidents, or the ostensibly masculine leaders of fashionable society. He knew that the people who dwell in courts and alleys and unfashionable streets outnumber ten to one those who live in brown-stone and marble palaces—and outvote them all the time. And he knew methods of appealing to the more numerous classes far more effectively than by speeches, or public meetings, or the publication in the newspapers of cards signed by "thousands of our business men and best citizens."

In company with some local Leader familia[r] with the people, he visited every bar-room i[n] every Election District, having previousl[y] notified the proprietor to inform as many o[f] the workers as he could reach that the Hon[-] orable Michael Mulhooly would be at th[e] saloon on such an evening, to meet and con[-] sult with his friends.

He endeavored to convince those whom h[e] thus met that he was qualified for a seat i[n] the Congress of the United States, by treat[-] ing and drinking with them every five min[-] utes, and by assuring them, during the shor[t] intervals between drinks, of his intention t[o] take care of "the boys," and by promisin[g] innumerable appointments, from $3,000 clerk[-] ships in the Treasury Department down t[o] the less responsible employment as day la[-] borer in the Custom-House. He well kne[w] that these were arguments which proved hi[s] fitness for Congressional honors far mor[e] conclusively than the most learned discus[-] sion of national issues. He seldom left [a] bar-room without the most satisfactory assu[r-] ances of the success of his arguments; thes[e] assurances being conveyed to him through such expressions as "Three cheers for our next Congressman," "You bet the boys are all with you," and "We're solid for Mike Mulhooly all the time."

[The use of such arguments Henry Armor and his friends did not understand.]

Thus he spent his nights, seldom reaching his bed until near day-break. But his most scientific work was done in the day-time, when, with the assistance of Blossom Brick, the other Leaders and the Boss, he endeavored to make sure that those whom he saw at night should be "solid for Mike Mulhooly all the time," by preventing them from being anything else. This was done by selecting the delegates who were to run in each Election District, and by setting right the officers who were to conduct the primary elections. It is in this kind of work that a genius for leadership is displayed to the greatest advantage.

To pick out a man who can be relied on, and who can carry his Election District against all opposition; to select a man who can induce the opposition to run him in a District which they are certain to carry, and who will betray them when he enters the Convention; to make such arrangements with the election officers that a District which cannot be carried in any way will yet return friendly delegates,—these are the strategic movements which betray political generalship, and show that the master-hand of the great Leader, or the greater Boss, has not been idle. These are the scientific movements on the political chess-board, by which pawns are made knights and bishops and queens before the movement is discovered by the adversary, and which decide political battles. And that political chess-pawn whose scruples prevent him from jumping a square contrary to the laws of the game, when the Great Player indicates that He wishes such an advantage of position, need not hope for reward or favor. His usefulness on the political chess-board is ended.

[Of this kind of political chess-playing Henry Armor and his friends had no knowledge.]

But the most important part of the contest yet remained to be accomplished. The temporary chairman who would organize the Convention had not yet been elected, and to capture him was to hold the key to the situation; for, in the language of Blossom Brick, *The temporary chairman is the Convention. He's an 8 to 7 man all the time.*"

If a candidate has failed to elect a majority of the delegates, but has secured the temporary chairman, it is his own fault, or that of the person selected for that position, if he does not secure the nomination.

Under the Rules, that officer was elected by the members of the City Committee from the five Wards which constituted the Congressional District. It was, therefore, necessary to make sure that three of these five Committee-men would vote for John O'Doyle, an ex-member of the Legislature, with large experience in organizing Conventions, and at present a Street Commissioner, who had been selected for this responsible position by Michael Mulhooly. The gentlemen upon whom the duty of making this selection devolved were—

1. Tim. O'Hoolahan.
2. Owen McPeak.
3. Daniel McGrody.
4. Dominick McTee.
5. James Sullivan.

O'Hoolahan at this time held a position in the Department of Sewers, but was in the interest of Hon. Charles Chauncey Chumbleson, and it was understood that he was prepared to purchase the temporary chairman with cash, if it could be done within reasonable limits.

McPeak was the member from Michael Mulhooly's Ward and had been recently appointed by him to a clerkship in the Treasurer's office, and could therefore be relied on.

McGrody was an assistant engineer in the Department of Fires, but, having been discharged from a situation in the Department of Taxes, about a year before, for acting contrary to Blossom Brick's orders, it was doubtful whether he could be induced to vote for any one in whom Blossom Brick was interested.

McTee was an appointee of the Boss in the Department of Public Buildings, but it was feared that O'Hoolahan would secure his vote with money, even if he had to give up his situation, which paid him only a small salary. Sullivan had recently been discharged from the Department of Health, and was at this time a candidate for the nomination for the Municipal Legislature.

McPeak's vote was, therefore, the only one which could be relied on. It was absolutely necessary to secure two more votes, and, to guard against accidents, an additional vote, if possible.

When a member of the City Committee finds that his vote is indispensable, he naturally places a high value upon it and takes advantage of the situation. And now began a series of interviews and negotiations as delicate and as guardedly conducted on both sides, as those diplomatic interviews between the representatives of great powers, upon which hang the fate of empires.

Sullivan was offered, first, a $2,000 clerkship in the Department of Water, which he refused; then, an Inspectorship in the Department of Streets, with opportunities to make *aliunde* $5,000 a year, which he also refused; and, finally, when nothing else would satisfy him, he was assured of the nomination which he desired, whereupon he agreed to vote for any person whom the Boss might name, and promised to be forever afterwards His most dutiful servant.

McTee was sent for and told what was expected of him, whereupon he declared that he couldn't support his family on the small salary he was getting, and intended to resign. He was told to do so, and left, swearing that he was "agin Mike Mulhooly all the time." A day or two later, however, he was again sent for, and upon being offered the $2,000 clerkship in the Department of Water, which had been refused by Sullivan, gladly accepted it, and swore that he had been "solid for Mulhooly all the time." Thus three votes were now promised; but, in order that no mistake might be made, a brother of McGrody was given a place in the Department of Parks as an overseer of laborers, and thus a fourth vote was secured.

The five Committee-men met and elected Hon. John O'Doyle temporary Chairman to organize the Convention.

[Of these diplomatic interviews and of this strategic movement Henry Armor and his friends knew nothing.]

To judge from the talk one heard in counting-houses, in the private offices of bank-presidents, at the club, and on the church steps, the nomination of Henry Armor was inevitable. It was universally agreed by all the good people one met in such places that his popularity was so great, his capacity so well known, his character so spotless, and the propriety of placing him where his great talents could be devoted to the good of his country, so manifest, that the mere suggestion of his candidacy was equivalent to a positive assurance of his triumphant election over all opposition.

The primary elections were duly held, and after a careful canvass of the results, it was claimed by Mr. Armor's friends that he had certainly elected sixty-one out of the ninety-seven delegates, or twelve more than were necessary to nominate him, after conceding all doubtful and contested Election Districts to his two opponents.

It had not been expected that the combined opposition would show so much strength, but the result was in every way most satisfactory, and his nomination on the next day but one was considered a foregone conclusion.

XVI.

The Convention.

WHEN the hour for the Convention to assemble came it was found that Michael Mulhooly's friends had possession of the Hall, and that the doorkeepers, who had been appointed by the temporary chairman, refused to admit any delegates except those whose names appeared upon a printed list, which had been prepared by the Chairman of the City Committee.

It was found that by this manœuvre but forty-two of the Armor delegates, or seven less than a majority, were admitted to the room. Those who were refused admission were told that they would have to go before the Committee on Contested Seats, which would be appointed immediately after the calling of the Convention to order, when they might, if they could, establish to the satisfaction of the Committee their right to sit as delegates.

Promptly at 11 o'clock the temporary Chairman rapped sharply on the table and declared that he had been delegated by the City Committee, in accordance with section 1 of Rule III., to organize the Convention, and he thereupon appointed as temporary secretaries John McNulty and Michael Dugan. The Chairman then directed one of the secretaries to call the roll from the printed list which had been prepared by the Chairman and secretaries of the City Committee.

An examination of this printed list showed the Armor men that, according to their reports, the names of nineteen Armor delegates had been left off, and the names of nineteen Mulhooly men placed on the list in place of those omitted.

Honorable Ingersole Aspenwall, a venerable gentleman who had represented his government at two European Courts, took the floor and courteously called the Chairman's attention to the fact that there were several

THE CONVENTION.

mistakes made in the names of the delegates from his own Ward; that in the seventh Election District the name of Patrick Dugan, who had received but seventy-three of the votes cast, had been inadvertently substituted for that of Mr. Howard Fielding, for whom one hundred and twenty-two votes had been polled, and to whom the election officers had given the certificate; and also that the name of Mr. Brantley Livingstone, who had been elected in the thirteenth Election District without opposition, was not to be found on the printed list, but in its place he found the name of Dennis Mooley, who had not been mentioned as a candidate, or even voted for.

Here a gentleman, evidently laboring under great excitement, and brandishing his arms in a threatening manner, said, "Mr. Prisidint, it's a dom'd lie, and it's misilf, Dennis Mooly, as knows it an' sez it; and'll trow ony mon out of the wundy that sez I'm not a dacintly ilicted diligate. I'm fur Mike Mulhooly, and that's wat's the mather."

The speaker continued to brandish his

arms, but his voice was drowned in the vociferous cheers for Mr. Mulhooly.

"Mr. Chairman," continued Mr. Aspenwall, not noticing the threat to throw him out of the "wundy," "I cannot suppose that these irregularities and mistakes were intentionally made by the Chairman of the City Committee, but——"

THE CHAIRMAN: "For the information of the gentleman the secretary will read Section 5 of Rule IV."

The secretary read as follows:

"Section 5. The election officers of each Election District shall, on the day after the primary election, furnish duplicate returns of the votes cast for delegates to the Chairman and secretaries of the City Committee, who shall sit at the Committee Rooms between the hours of 12 M. and 2 P. M. on that day for the purpose of receiving such returns; and they shall from the duplicate returns so presented to them make up a list of the delegates who appear to have been elected to each Convention, and shall furnish a printed copy of said list to the Temporary Chairman of such Convention before 9 o'clock of the day for holding the Convention, which list shall be the roll of the Convention until corrected by the adoption of the report of the Committee on Contested Seats."

THE CHAIRMAN: "The gentleman will, therefore, see that if such mistakes as he alludes to have been made, the Chair is powerless to correct them, but they must be passed upon by the Committee on Contested Seats, which will be selected in the manner prescribed by the Rules as soon as the secretary has finished calling the roll."

MR. ASPENWALL: "But the Chair must see that the gentlemen who have been regularly elected—nineteen of them, I am informed—have not only been excluded from the Hall, but they have not even been notified of this action, or that there is any dispute about their right to their seats; and, therefore, they came here without having given the notice required by the Rules to entitle them to appear as contestants, and without having prepared the requisite petition to entitle them to be heard by the Committee. But what is still worse is that nineteen other gentlemen, some of whom were not even voted for by the people, have been placed on the roll as delegates, have been admitted to the Hall, are allowed to participate in drawing the Committee on Contested Seats, and, as no notice has been served that their seats are contested, may even sit on that Committee and refuse to hear those whose seats they have wrongfully taken. The manifest unfairness, injustice and irregularity of such a proceeding must——"

THE CHAIRMAN: "The gentleman is out of order. The Chair does not make the Rules. Its only duty is to interpret and enforce them, and that it proposes to do fairly and honestly."

MR. ASPENWALL: "I move the appointment of a Committee——"

THE CHAIRMAN: "The gentleman is again out of order. Under the order of business laid down in Section 2 of Rule V., no motion, except to take a recess, is in order until the report of the Committee on Contested Seats has been made to the Convention. The Chair will be compelled to refuse to recognize any gentleman until the calling of the roll is finished. The secretary will proceed with the call of the roll."

When the secretary had finished several gentlemen attempted to call attention to the omission of the names of regularly-elected delegates and the substitution of others, and great confusion and excitement followed. For fully fifteen minutes the Chairman continued to pound on the table with a hammer which he used for a gavel, and tried to persuade the delegates to take their seats. For some time it looked as if a detachment of police would have to be sent for to clear the Hall. Finally, in a temporary lull, the Chairman succeeded in announcing that the first business in order was the selection of the Committee on Contested Seats, and directed the secretary to read Section 3 of Rule V., which was in these words:

"Section 3. Immediately after the calling of the roll has been concluded, a committee of seven delegates, to whom shall be referred, without debate, all questions relative to contested seats in the convention, shall be drawn in the following manner:

"The secretaries shall write upon separate slips of paper of equal size the names of all delegates whose seats are uncontested (and no delegate's seat shall be considered as contested unless the notice provided for in Section 8 of Rule IV. shall have been given), and when the slips shall have been thus prepared, they shall be handed to the temporary Chairman, and be by him examined and counted, and if he shall find them to be correct, he shall then place them in a hat or box and see that they are thoroughly shaken and mixed together. One secretary shall then draw a slip from the hat or box and hand it to the temporary Chairman, who shall announce the name appearing thereon to the Convention, which name shall be forthwith recorded by the other secretary. Any delegate may then peremptorily challenge the right of the person so drawn to serve upon said committee, whereupon the name so challenged shall be marked 'Challenged.' Another slip shall then be drawn, and the name thereon announced and recorded, and so on, until but seven slips remain in the hat, when the seven slips so remaining shall be handed to the temporary Chairman, who shall announce the names which appear thereon as the members of the Committee on Contested Seats, and no challenge shall be allowed to any of the said seven names so drawn."

This rule had been recently adopted because the old rule, which allowed the temporary Chairman to appoint this Committee, was found to invariably result in the selection of a Committee *wholly* in the interest of the candidate favored by the temporary Chairman, and in the unseating of a sufficient number of delegates by the Committee to secure a majority in favor of the fortunate candidate.

In theory, the new rule was admitted to be perfectly fair, as it left the selection of the Committee almost entirely to chance. But persons were not wanting who contended that its practical operation was no better than that of the old rule, which made the temporary Chairman "an 8 to 7 man all the time." They alleged that this rule was only used as a screen, behind which to perpetrate the old-fashioned frauds, and that the Chairman and Secretaries invariably managed to draw a majority of the Committee favorable to their candidate. They contended that it was the easiest thing in the world to do so by giving the seven slips previously agreed upon some slight peculiarity of size, shape or color, or by miscalling the names, or by secreting these slips under the hat-band or in the sleeve—tricks which could be easily performed without danger of discovery by one not possessing the skill of a sleight-of hand performer. Of course, these complaints were always made by defeated and disappointed candidates.

The drawing then proceeded according to the rule, and resulted in the selection of the following persons, viz.:

Fred. M. Finnel, an Armor delegate.
James Smith, " " "
Edward Whitley, a Chumbleson delegate.
James Kelly, " Mulhooly "
Patrick Donohue, " " "
John McGinnis, " " "
Terrence McGlue, " " "

The Committee, therefore, stood four for Mulhooly, two for Armor, and one for Chumbleson. The Armor and Chumbleson delegates had never before been in a Convention, and knew nothing of their duties as members of such a Committee, while the Mulhooly men were experts. All four held positions in Departments controlled by the Boss, and could be relied upon not to lose a trick.

The Committee immediately retired, and, after selecting James Kelly as Chairman, announced that they would hear all persons claiming seats in the Convention, including those who had not given notice or prepared petitions according to the Rules. This spirit of fair dealing was highly commended. They were in session for nearly two hours, and finally reported in favor of the sitting delegates, and consequently against the nineteen Armor delegates, who had been prevented from entering the Hall. The Armor members made a minority report, but the Convention adopted the report of the majority by a vote of fifty-one to forty-six, and by the same vote elected Hon. Samuel Snort President, and made the temporary secretaries officers of the Convention.

The Convention being thu organized, the

President announced that nominations were now in order, and called for the pledges required of candidates by Section 9 of Rule V., which was in these words:

"Section 9. No candidate shall be placed in nomination or voted for in any Convention, until he shall have signed and filed with the Chairman the following written pledge, which shall be in all cases read to the Convention:

"I pledge my honor that I will abide by the decision of this Convention, and will support its nominee or nominees; and that I will not under any circumstances run as an independent candidate, or permit my name to be used as a candidate for the office of ——, by any other party, association, meeting or committee."

The pledges of Mr. Michael Mulhooly and Hon. Charles Chauncey Chumbleson were then handed up and read, but no response was made to the call for Mr. Armor's pledge.

Hon. Emanuel Fairweather then nominated Hon. Michael Mulhooly, and paid a glowing tribute to his personal worth, his party service, and his spotless record in the Municipal Legislature.

Hon. Charles Chauncey Chumbleson was also nominated, but the name of Henry Armor was not mentioned.

A ballot was immediately taken, which resulted as follows:

        Mulhooly, 51.
        Chumbleson, 4.

The Armor delegates did not vote. The President then declared that the Honorable Michael Mulhooly had received fifty-one votes, and as this was a majority of all the delegates present, and a majority of forty-seven of all the votes cast, he was duly nominated as the candidate of the party for Congress from that District.

A committee was thereupon appointed to wait upon the candidate and announce to him the action of the Convention. They found him in Tim O'Leary's saloon across the street, and when, five minutes later, they entered the Hall, Terrence McGlue leading him by one arm, and Patrick Donohue by the other, the enthusiasm of the Convention knew no bounds. Delegates stood upon chairs and benches, waving their hats and cheering for "Mike Mulhooly" for fully fifteen minutes, while the Armor delegates sat in sullen silence, and the successful candidate stood bowing and smiling at the front of the platform and endeavoring to obtain a hearing. Finally, when the excitement had in a measure subsided, he spoke as follows:

"I'm proud of this unexpected honor, and I thank yez all for it. As it was unsolicited on my part, I feel the honor you've done me in nominating me for Congress. Ony man might be proud of it. And I'm not ashamed to say I am proud of it. [Cheers.] I'm not a public speaker, but I'm one of the bye's, and, what's more, I'm for the bye's all the time. [Cheer after cheer greeted this utterance.] And I mane, if ilicted, to take care of the bye's all the time. [This brave and manly declaration of principles provoked still greater enthusiasm.] I point to my past record for the truth of what I say. And so, thanking you once more, I'll be glad to see yez all across the way, at Tim O'Leary's saloon."

Having reached his climax, like a true orator, he bowed and retired. When he reached the floor he was surrounded by his devoted followers, who were anxious to shake hands with their next Congressman, who was not ashamed to say he was one of the "bye's" and "for the bye's all the time." They followed him across the way to Tim O'Leary's, where case after case of wine was opened, and the rejoicings over their great victory lasted all through the day and late into the night.

Thus Michael Mulhooly was nominated in strict accordance with the Rules of his party. According to all its traditions, he had won his nomination fairly, was entitled to the support of every true party-man, and to have voted against him would have been the unpardonable political sin.

Nevertheless, the same afternoon the sixty-one Armor delegates who claimed to have been elected, met, organized and adopted a resolution, denouncing the proceedings of the regular Convention held in the morning, and declaring that Henry Armor, Esq., was the regular nominee of the party in the District for Congress.

XVII.

The Voice of the Press.

THOSE newspapers which the Reformers claimed belonged to, or were controlled by, the Ring, indorsed the nomination of Michael Mulhooly in the most earnest manner. They spoke of him as the regular nominee of the party, and referred to the Armor delegates as "kickers" and "bolters," and dismissed their Convention and their nomination as unworthy of consideration.

The Argus-Eyed said:

"Michael Mulhooly, the regular nominee of the party, is a man of the people, who, by industry and perseverance, has risen from an humble station to a position which any man in this great city might feel proud to hold. His career in the Municipal Legislature gives assurance that he will not misrepresent his District in the National Legislature, and we predict his election by a magnificent majority."

The DAWN OF DAY said:

"It is seldom that a party Convention so well expresses the party's will. The people of this Congressional District desired the nomination of Mr. Michael Mulhooly because they had tried him and found him in every way worthy of their confidence. They felt that his abilities and public services merited this recognition, and that his experience in public affairs peculiarly qualified him for the higher and broader field of national politics. We say, Gentlemen of the Convention, well done!"

The BOSS'S OWN said:

"No man in this District is better qualified for a seat in Congress than Mr. Michael Mulhooly. He was our choice first, last and all the time, and the action of the Convention is, therefore, gratifying to us."

The VOICE OF THE PEOPLE said:

"That Mr. Michael Mulhooly is worthy of this new honor no one who knows him will doubt or question. That he will be elected by a majority which will be a credit to himself and to his District, we feel sure. The people of this country are at last commencing to understand the difference between practical statesmanship that brings forth fruit and the barren political Miss-Nancyism, of which Mr. Henry Armor, who received the empty honor of a so-called nomination by a few 'kickers,' is a fitting representative."

The PUBLIC WATCH-DOG, after paying a high tribute to the distinguished talents of the regular nominees, said:

"The action of the score or two of kickers who, after participating in the proceedings of the Convention and finding themselves hopelessly in the minority, proceeded to hold a Convention and nominate a candidate of their own, would be unworthy of notice were it not that such action is always a dangerous precedent, which should not go unrebuked. No man has a right to ask to be sent as a delegate to a Convention who is not willing to be governed by the party rules, and to abide by the decision of the majority. No man is fit to be candidate who will encourage such dishonorable conduct on the part of his delegates. Fidelity to the party is a duty which every good citizen owes to his party for the sake of its principles, and in order to assure its success; and that duty is not discharged by fidelity only when the action of the party is in accordance with our individual wishes or preferences. If the minority is to be encouraged to bolt as soon as it discovers that it is the minority party, organization is at an end, and party success a matter of chance. We trust that a rule will be adopted compelling every delegate, before he receives his credentials, to remain in the Convention and abide by the decision of the majority, whatever that decision may be."

Such was public sentiment as reflected in all the journals of the city, except one.

The TRUTH-TELLER, a journal which catered to the tastes of those people who sympathized with the Reform movement, after complimenting the seceding delegates on the manliness and independence of character which they had displayed, and indorsing their nominee as one pre-eminently worthy of public trust, and pre-eminently qualified to represent his District, said:

. . . "But who, on the other hand, is the Ring

candidate for a seat in the Congress of the United States of America, and what his antecedents? No honest man can answer that question truthfully without a blush of shame. But it is a question which must be asked and must be answered without mincing words.

"A bog-trotter by birth ; a waif washed up on our shores ; a scullion-boy in a gin-mill frequented by thieves and shoulder-hitters ; afterwards a bartender in and subsequently the proprietor of this low groggery ; a repeater before he was of age ; a rounder, bruiser and shoulder-hitter ; then made an American citizen by fraud after a residence of but two years ; a leader of a gang of repeaters before the ink on his fraudulent naturalization papers was dry ; then a —— ——'s —— ; then a corrupt and perjured election officer ; then for years a corrupt and perjured member of the Municipal Legislature, always to be hired or bought by the highest bidder, and always an uneducated, vulgar, flashily-dressed, obscene creature of the Ring which made him what he is, and of which he is a worthy representative ; such, in brief, is the man who has been forced upon the party, by the most shameless frauds, as its candidate for the American Congress. This is filthy language, but it is the only way in which to describe the filthy subject to which it refers, and every man who reads it must admit that it is only the simple truth.

"Is it possible that the American people are compelled to scour the gutter, the gin-mill and the brothel for a candidate for Congress? Is it possible that the Ring which has already plundered the city for so many years, and which has so long abused our patience with its arbitrary nominations of the most unworthy people, for the most honorable and responsible offices, will be permitted to crown its infamies by sending to Congress this creature, who represents nothing decent, and nothing fit to be named to decent ears?

"There is one point of view, however, in which this nomination, monstrous as it is, may prove to be a public blessing. It will provoke the people to throw off the yoke of this Ring of Confederated Thieves under which they have patiently staggered and groaned for years. It will show them that, monstrous as Ring-rule is, as a scheme of plunder, it is more monstrous as a despotism which makes of free people its slaves, and laughs at the shame and stripes it puts upon them. It will show them that the notorious Blossom Brick told the simple truth when he said 'party rules are the reins and party spirit the bit by which We drive the people.' It will force the American

INGRATITUDE.—p. 139.

Copyrighted, 1889, by Gebbie & Co.

people to rise in their majesty and say to each one of these Bosses—the worst of whom are always uneducated, unscrupulous and characterless foreigners—we invited you here to find a refuge, not to build an empire; we welcomed you as strangers, not as rulers; we adopted you as citizens and in return you have made us slaves, and have fattened upon us for years, and have kicked us when we dared to ask for but an equal share with yourselves in the control of this, our own government; but the end has come. Go! Choose between the obscurity from which you came and the prisons which your crimes have prepared for you. Choose, but choose quickly!"

This article produced a profound impression upon the Leaders, the Ring and the Boss, if it did not greatly disturb the people. It meant business and threatened danger.

XVIII.

Trouble.

AT noon that day a conference of the Leaders and the Boss was held at His private office. They looked at each other significantly, and each waited for the other to speak. Finally, some one hurled a verbal thunderbolt at the editor of the libelous sheet. Then another and another followed in quick succession. Their wrath was like that mighty wrath that raged upon Olympus when the Giants dared to assail it and disturb its serenity with their clamor.

Then Blossom Brick uttered those memorable words:—

"IF THE PEOPLE EVER TUMBLE TO OUR GAME—HELL WILL BE TO PAY!"

His practical mind did not waste itself in impotent wrath. He looked forward to the possible results which this publication might bring about. He saw in it more than an insult; it was a menace. It meant rebellion. The people, the "blind asses" as he was wont to call them, are never dangerous so long as they are deceived, but he knew how great the danger is from the moment when they begin "to kick." His suggestion commanded instant attention. The sense of insult was forgotten in the sense of danger which settled down upon them like an invisible cloud. They began to realize that their power was in danger, that their rule was threatened, that their gigantic schemes for the public good might come to naught if such public utterances were allowed to be repeated with impunity. They said, "If this licentiousness of the press is not speedily rebuked and curbed, which one of us will be safe?"

Then they sent for their candidate Michael Mulhooly, whose ambition had brought all this trouble upon them. He came, as slick, oily, rotund and smiling as ever. He had read the ARGUS-EYED, the DAWN OF DAY, the BOSS'S OWN, the VOICE OF THE PEOPLE and the

Public Watch-Dog, but he had not read the Truth-teller. It was shown to him. He took it up with a smile, which gradually faded from his face. He laid the paper down and was evidently not pleased with what he had read. He looked first at one, then at another, and finally at his watch, and said, "If I can find the —— —— —— —— —— —— ——

—— —— —— —— —— —— —— ——

I'll put a head on him!" He made the too common mistake of supposing that when one has been charged with crime by a newspaper, the best way to disprove the charge is to "put a head on" the editor.

Then they sent for their favorite lawyer, Theoptolimus Sly, Esq., a small man with a big voice, who was certain to make at least as much noise in the world as a dinner-gong. He came promptly, in obedience to orders, as he always did, and comforted them with the assurance that the article was undoubtedly a libel, and that the editor could be arrested for it.

Then the Boss Himself sent a messenger for Judge Coke, whom he had "made," and who wanted to be re-"made" shortly. He, too, came in obedience to orders, as he, too, always did. He was closeted with the Boss for an hour, and, after he had gone, the Boss said, "I've fixed it." This was another decree of Fate.

That afternoon Mr. Carson Cleaver, the editor-in-chief of the *Truth-teller*, was arrested on the charge of libel, and held to bail in the sum of $2,000. A bill of indictment was immediately sent before the Grand Jury and returned "a true bill," and Theoptolimus Sly, Esq., announced that the defendant would be tried the next day and "railroaded," a technical term of the Sessions, which signifies a modern mode of administering justice so expeditiously that one accused of crime is arrested, tried, convicted, sentenced and put at a felon's work-bench before he has time to sneeze or to say, "God bless me, where am I?"

Judge Coke, however, was not on the bench the next morning—his term was not to commence until the following Monday—and the defendant, Mr. Carson Cleaver, was notified that his case would not be called for trial that day, but would be tried, God willing, on the following Monday. Thus the impending sword of Justice was temporarily stayed.

XIX.

Justice.

ON Monday Mr. Carson Cleaver appeared in court with his counsel. Mr. Michael Mulhooly also appeared with his counsel. In addition to Mr. Theoptolimus Sly, there had been retained to assist the District Attorney—another Boss-made administrator of Justice, whose life was rendered miserable by his fear of newspaper criticism on the one hand, and his dread of Boss disfavor on the other hand—two distinguished criminal lawyers—Mr. Gandy Grip and Mr. Bowles Bowser.

Gandy Grip was a leader in his profession. He had come to the bar with meagre educational and social advantages, but possessing what proved to be of much greater value to him—a profound knowledge of the criminal classes and their habits, derived from his early associations, and an exceptional capacity for attracting clients, which insured his success. This rare business tact was at once displayed by his giving a supper to all the court officers and deputy-sheriffs of his acquaintance, which resulted in establishing so good an understanding between them that they recommended him to all criminals who came under their charge, and he divided with them all the fees which he was thus enabled to earn. The worldly wisdom of this arrangement was speedily demonstrated by the fact that when older lawyers than himself were still wrestling hopelessly with the problem of how to pay office rent out of office receipts, he was enjoying a lucrative practice, and carrying on his person and in his pockets diamonds enough to have stocked a jewelry store, received from clients with more diamonds than cash. In a short time his reputation became so firmly established that no thief or burglar in the city would go to work with any degree of confidence without first ascertaining that Gandy Grip was in town, and that his services could be secured at a moment's notice. He could demolish a witness by a single question, and his powers of vituperation were so transcendent that the critical audiences who frequented the Sessions placed him in the front rank of living orators. He confined himself exclusively to criminal or quasi-criminal practice, and would not enter a common pleas or an equity court without having first procured an introduction to the presiding judge. He knew better than any detective on the force how to recover stolen bonds, and in doubtful divorce cases he was regarded as the highest living authority. But he was pre-eminently great in securing verdicts. When he was engaged in the trial of a case there was not a sporting man in town who would not give long odds that if he did not get a verdict, he would at least secure a disagreement of the jury.

Bowles Bowser, his colleague, was also a criminal lawyer of note. Having no taste for office practice, he found that he could more advantageously employ his office hours in the neighboring bar-rooms, studying human nature, than in poring over abstruse and contradictory law books. Whilst he was, therefore, somewhat weak in legal knowledge, he was surprisingly great in disorderly house cases. Had there been a defect in the pleadings large enough to have allowed a circus band wagon to be driven through it with ease, he would probably not have found it in a lifetime with the aid of a microscope; but his skill in "fixing" juries was so perfect that older lawyers frequently retained him as a silent colleague on account of this exceptional talent.

It was evident, therefore, that the prosecutor meant business.

As soon as Judge Coke had settled himself comfortably in his seat, and the clerk had satisfied himself as to the condition of his voice by calling over the list of jurors, the counsel for the prosecutor advanced to the bar of the court—Mr. Sly in advance, and as eager as a dinner-gong to make himself heard; Mr. Bowser following, and nodding encouragingly to a juror of his acquaintance; and Mr. Grip bringing up the rear and unlimbering his heaviest guns for the engagement; and one after another reminded the court—although it was the first day of Judge Coke's term—that the case of The People against Carson Cleaver had been fixed for trial, and that they desired that the defendant might be at once arraigned and required to plead, so that the case could proceed to trial without delay.

The court having been satisfied by the assurances of three such eminent counsel, and by an encouraging but nervous nod from the District Attorney, that Mr. Carson Cleaver ought to be called upon to answer as to the wrong he stood charged with having done the people, instructed the clerk to interrogate him upon this subject. This duty the clerk proceeded to discharge with his most tremendous frown and in the very lowest notes of his register, believing that no criminal, however hardened, could endure this terrible ordeal without confessing his guilt; and he looked both shocked and disappointed when Mr. Carson Cleaver, in a tone of cool indifference, replied, "Not guilty," without even looking at him.

Before the clerk had entirely recovered his breath and his countenance, the counsel for the defendant rose up and said that his client was unprepared for trial, although anxious for it; that he proposed to sustain his plea of "Not guilty" by proving that the prosecutor himself was guilty of all the crimes with which he had been charged in the alleged libelous publication, and that as he would be compelled to summon a very large number of witnesses in order to establish every charge he had made, he would require a week for this preparation, and would willingly appear on the next Monday and make good his charges or take the consequences.

This application, as well as the implied assault upon the integrity of their client, so incensed the prosecutor's counsel that they endeavored to address the court in chorus and to demonstrate that the application was nothing less than the most monstrous attempt to trifle with Justice that had ever been witnessed by each of them individually, and by all of them collectively, in a court of Justice. Finally, when these gentlemen had ridden down the defendant and the defendant's counsel, and trampled over each other in their precipitate charge upon the court, to prevent it from permitting Justice to be trifled with in its presence, Judge Coke looked encouragingly at the District Attorney, who, finding that some effort was also expected of him to defeat this contemplated attempt to trifle with Justice, timidly suggested that as the defendant had been notified on the preceding Wednesday that his case would be tried on this day, and had, therefore, had five days in which to prepare, and had made no attempt whatever to prepare, it did, indeed, look like an attempt to trifle with Justice.

Judge Coke, who by this time seemed to have some suspicion that there was really an intention on the part of some one to trifle with Justice, and in his own presence, too, remarked, angrily, that as no "legal" ground had been laid for a continuance, he thought the counsel for the prosecution were right, and that the application looked very much like an attempt to trifle with Justice. Warming up with his subject, he continued, that "when an editor publishes so gross a libel on a citizen, and especially on one so favorably known to the community and to the court, he ought to be prepared to prove the truth of his foul charges on the spot, or to take the consequences. He was certainly entitled to no *favors* from the court." Whereupon, throwing back his head angrily against the back of his chair, he ordered the trial to proceed.

The counsel for the defendant made another attempt to procure delay, but was promptly rebuked by the court for his repeated attempts to trifle with Justice, and was ordered to " go on," whereupon he sat down.

The clerk, having pulled himself together after his first discomfiture, looked at the defendant with an expression which indicated that he meant to be even with him and to break his stubborn spirit before he was through with him, and proceeded to call a jury. As each juror approached the box the counsel for the prosecution put their heads together and looked first at a paper which they took care to conceal, and then at the juror, and if they did not apparently find the juror to their liking, one of them whispered to the District Attorney, who nervously requested the juror to "stand aside"—this being a privilege which the law still gives that officer in cases in which he is determined to convict, and, therefore, prefers what Blossom Brick called a "solid jury."

In this manner the calling of the jury proceeded until the following twelve men were chosen, viz.:

1. Patrick McGlaughlin.
2. James McShane.
3. John McTighe.
4. James McRody.
5. Timothy McMunn.
6. John McGuiggan.
7. Dennis McShiel.
8. Michael McFinn.
9. John McGittigen.
10. Larry McQuade.
11. James McAtee.
12. James McNamara.

The challenges on both sides having been

exhausted, nothing remained to do but to swear the jury, whereupon the clerk, casting another reproachful glance at the defendant as if he meant to assure him that he would yet regret his hardness of heart, in the most solemn and impressive manner administered the oath to "well and truly try the issue joined between the People and Carson Cleaver, the defendant, and a true verdict to give, according to the evidence, so help you God!"

Then Bowles Bowser winked significantly to Gandy Grip, and Blossom Brick whispered to the Boss, "Solid all the time!" Theoptolimus Sly subsequently told the District Attorney that he need not be afraid that the defendant had "got any work in on them," as five of the jury were in public employment, and the other seven were, as he was assured by Mr. Grip and Mr. Bowser, "all right."

The District Attorney then arose, and in a somewhat embarrassed and nervous manner stated the nature of the crime which the defendant was charged with having committed against the people, and sat down, evidently greatly relieved. To prove the publication, two witnesses were called, who testified that they knew the defendant to be the editor of the TRUTH-TELLER, and that they had bought copies of the issue of the newspaper which contained the libelous article, which they had also read, and understood to refer to the prosecutor.

Then Mr. Michael Mulhooly was called, and, leaving his seat, he stepped into the witness-box, drew off his yellow kid gloves, smiled at the judge, bowed encouragingly to the jury, and solemnly swore to tell the truth, the whole truth, and nothing but the truth, *so help him God!* He took up the copy of the newspaper by one corner, as though he feared it would soil his hands if he took a fair hold of it, and declared that he had read the libelous article, and, so far as it related to himself, there was not one single word of truth in it from beginning to end, but that it was an infamous lie, as everybody who knew him could not help but know.

He then turned with a defiant air towards the counsel for the defendant, who, to the astonishment of everybody, declined to ask any questions. It had been expected that he would attempt to riddle the prosecutor by a rapid fire of questions, as damaging as a discharge of grape and canister, in reference to where he came from and how he knew it; how old he was and who told him so; what he did for a living and how he managed to do it; what crimes he had been guilty of and how he had got out of prison, and similar questions, such as prosecutors are accustomed to look for from those gentlemen, who are specially sworn to see to it that no attempt to trifle with Justice shall ever succeed, where they can prevent such a misfortune from happening to her.

When the prosecutor's counsel announced that they had closed their case, the counsel for the defendant told the jury that he had hundreds of witnesses to call, but that they were not in the court-room, because the prosecutor was so anxious to have his character vindicated that he insisted upon a trial when he knew they were all absent. He added that he would ask the jury to say, that no editor should ever be called upon to answer the charge of libel, for a publication concerning the official conduct of a public officer, or the character of a candidate for a high and honorable office, until he has been given a decent opportunity to be heard by his witnesses; —that no man who claims to be libeled, and is unwilling to give his adversary a week in which to prove the truth of what has been published, is entitled to the sort of vindication which a verdict, under such circumstances, would give him. He therefore asked the jury to show their condemnation of this premature and indecent prosecution by promptly acquitting the defendant. And then, without another word, he sat down.

This extraordinary language evidently produced no effect upon the jurors; but the countenances of the court, of the counsel for the prosecution and of the prosecutor himself, showed that they now realized that they were indeed witnesses of an unmistakable attempt to trifle with Justice. Judge Coke looked as if he felt called upon to rebuke it immediately, and in the most decided manner.

Mr. Gandy Grip, however, came to the rescue of the court and of that blind goddess whom he so profoundly worshipped, and to whom he so frequently and so eloquently appealed, and proceeded to resent the insult which had been offered to her in his presence in a speech which was, beyond doubt, the greatest effort of his life. For two hours he poured forth a torrent of vituperation against the counsel for the defendant, the licentiousness of the press, and the unmanly and cowardly libeler who sat unmoved before him, which provoked repeated outbursts of applause from the crowd which filled every part of the court-room. Then, with the consummate art of the great orator, he turned to the innocent subject of this heartless libeler's calumny, and portrayed his early struggles with adversity; his slow but gradual steps towards a higher sphere than that in which he was born; his great public services; his many virtues; his high and honorable ambition, and his gradual ascent up the ladder of Fame, "Until," said he, "like Excelsior, he lies on the mountain top, 'midst the snow and ice of public scorn, frozen to the heart by this vile defamer's calumnious breath." This beautiful and pathetic figure of speech touched the hearts of his jury, and two or three commenced to use their pocket-handkerchiefs and the backs of their hands freely; while Michael Mulhooly was not ashamed to be seen wiping a tear from his manly eye. Then, having reached his hearers' hearts, in tones of withering scorn he dwelt upon the conduct of the defense in standing over the prostrate form of their victim and reiterating the false and wicked charges which they could not call a single living witness to substantiate.

When he closed no one present supposed that the defendant's counsel would attempt to reply.

But he rose up and spoke substantially as follows:

"I presume I need not call witnesses into the box to prove what every man on the jury knows. I need not call witnesses to tell you that this prosecution has been brought by a Ring of confederated thieves, who have ruled and plundered this city for years, for the purpose——"

Here Judge Coke interrupted him and said sharply, "Counsel must confine their remarks to the evidence in the case, and not refer to public rumor."

"What stronger evidence," continued the lawyer, "what stronger evidence is there in this very case that these rumors are true, and that what I say about the purpose of this prosecution is true, than that furnished by the indecent manner in which it has been forced to trial, and by the presence in this court-room of the very Chiefs of that Ring, who are the real prosecutors, seeking protection for themselves, and not vindication for this prosecutor?"

"I will not permit this line of argument," angrily interrupted the Judge.

"I am sorry that it displeases the court," replied the lawyer, "but I am compelled to discharge my duty to this defendant, irrespective of judicial pleasure or displeasure."

"Repeat it if you dare," said the Judge,

"and I'll forthwith commit you for contempt."

The lawyer bowed and continued, "It is not my duty to direct the court what it shall, or what it shall not do. But it is my duty to say to this jury all that in my conscience I believe ought to be said on behalf of my client about this case and its surroundings; and that I shall continue to say, respectfully, but fearlessly, whatever may be the consequences. I will, however, remind this honorable court that fair play is a part of the unwritten law of this land, and that no prosecutor can hurry a defendant to trial without his witnesses, and then ask that his motives shall not be commented upon by counsel, or considered by the jury as a part, and a most material part, of the case. And I will also remind this honorable court that the prosecutor and the defendant are not the only persons interested in this trial. Back of the prosecutor sit his friends, whom I arraign as the real prosecutors; and back of this court stands this great community, who will not permit wrong to be done in the name of Justice, and to whom, not only this jury, but also your Honor, must answer for the manner in which Justice is administered this day in this her sacred temple."

The Judge looked at him sternly for a moment, then resumed his pen, and the lawyer continued:

"I put it to the conscience of each man on this jury whether I have uttered one word but the simple truth. There is not a man in that box who does not know the political condition of this city and the manner in which it has been ruled and robbed for years by a band of political bandits, to which this prosecutor belongs, and which has the effrontery to come here and endeavor to force the conviction of an editor, in the absence of his witnesses, because he dared to attack them.

"I do not intend to discuss either this article, or the testimony of the prosecutor. Until you have been permitted to hear the defendant's witnesses you cannot determine whether he published a libel, or the truth. If he published a tissue of lies he deserves the severest penalty of the law. If he published the truth he deserves and will receive the thanks of the whole community. But you dare not convict him—you have no right to try him—when he stands here and says, 'Give me but one week and I will prove that every word I published about this man was the truth.'

"Would an innocent and wronged prosecutor, conscious of his innocence, and of his ability to establish it, in the face of such a challenge, insist upon a trial? Would he not rather say, 'I, too, am on trial. Take a week—take a month, if you need it,—and then I will meet you and prove that you have wronged me!' But when a prosecutor, who is a public officer and a candidate for a still higher office, runs into a court of Justice, hot, breathless, and trembling, and says, 'For God's sake convict this man before he can get the witnesses here to prove that I am a thief!' he ought to be lashed out of the court-room with whips made of the scorn and indignation of all honest jurors.

"Yet you are asked, in just such a case, to render a verdict of guilty against this defendant. I pity the man who lends himself to-day to such an act of injustice, and who must meet to-morrow, face to face, an outraged community, and answer for the manner in which he has kept his oath and discharged this great public duty."

Then Judge Coke charged the jury substantially as follows:

He said that the case was a perfectly simple one, and the duty of the jury so plain, that they could not go astray. If they believed the testimony for the prosecution—and he did not see how they could disbelieve it without violating their oaths—the defendant was guilty of publishing the wickedest libel he had ever read. No attempt was made to deny the publication, but the defendant, through his counsel, reiterated the vile charges in open court. Having had five days in which to prepare for his trial, he came into court without a single witness, and asked to be acquitted, not because his guilt had not been proved, but because the court had refused to grant any longer delay. It was seldom that a lawyer so far forgot his duty to himself and to the court, as to make such a shameful assault upon a prosecutor as that to which they had been compelled to listen. It was more than an outrage; it was an insult to the jury and to the court. He felt called upon to say thus much to the jury on the subject, and he would afterwards consider what further notice the court ought to take of what was nothing less than a gross contempt.

He then handed the bill of indictment to the jury, instructing them to do their duty like men and not to be intimidated by threats of public opinion.

The foreman took the bill from the clerk, looked at the rest of the jurymen, who nodded affirmatively, and then reported a verdict of "Guilty," which was recorded.

Judge Coke immediately ordered the defendant to stand up for sentence, whereupon his counsel again rose up and began,—"I desire to move——"

"Sit down, sir!" said Judge Coke. "You have grossly insulted the court and misbehaved as an attorney. I did not compel you to take your seat at the time, because you were addressing the jury on behalf of a defendant who was upon trial. But I will not permit you to address the court again in this case. If the defendant himself has anything further to add, I will hear him."

While the defendant and his counsel were conferring, the Boss sent to Mr. Theoptolimus Sly a slip of paper, on which he had written:—

"We'll spoil all. Tell Judge to allow motion for new trial and delay. Will explain."

Mr. Sly read it and handed it to Mr. Grip, who also read it, and passed it up to the Judge. He, too, read it and said, "If the purpose of the defendant's counsel was only to make the ordinary motion for a new trial, I will allow it to be made in writing, and filed with the clerk. In the meantime the defendant will renew his bail. Crier, adjourn the court!" Whereupon the crier declared that the court stood adjourned, and the Judge came down and shook hands with Michael Mulhooly, Blossom Brick and the Boss.

POLITICAL TWINS.

——"and the Judge came down and shook hands with Michael Mulhooly."—p. 166.

Copyrighted, 1889, by Gebbie & Co.

Thus Justice was done and Michael Mulhooly was vindicated. The verdict of a jury of his countrymen had declared that his character was as white and spotless as the ceiling of the temple of Justice itself, which had just been newly calcimined.

XX.

A Judge Challenged.

THE next morning in the *Truth-teller* appeared the following double-leaded leader:

JUDGES, HALT!!!

"Almost any evil in a Republic can be endured with some degree of patience except that of a corrupt or slavish Judiciary. When Judges, forgetful of their manhood and their oaths, lend themselves to oppression and become the pliant tools of tyrants, they may be very sure that the people will not be slow to redress such intolerable wrongs, and that they will, if forced to the extremity, enter the temple of Justice and tear down the dishonored and foresworn priests who have desecrated the sacred altars, and will trample them under foot in the mire of the streets. *Salus populi suprema est lex.*

A JUDGE CHALLENGED.

"This solemn warning is especially addressed to Judge Coke.

"It is within the personal knowledge of the editor and two of his friends that, immediately before the warrant for his arrest was issued, the head of the Ring sent a message for Judge Coke, who immediately went to the Boss's private office, where he remained closeted with him for nearly one hour. Did he go there in obedience to orders, to receive orders that the editor must be convicted at all hazards? What actually passed at that interview can be known only to Judge Coke himself, and to one other person. But immediately after the termination of that interview a warrant for libel was issued against the editor, and he was bound over, a bill at once sent before the Grand Jury, and the intimation given out of the intention on the part of prosecutors to 'railroad' him. For some reason, not difficult to understand when it is known that Judge Coke was not then upon the bench, and that his term would not begin until the next Monday, the case against the defendant was postponed until the very day upon which Judge

Coke's term began, and he was then immediately forced to trial, notwithstanding his demand for one week's time in which to procure his witnesses, and his solemn avowal that he would in exactly one week from that day appear and prove the truth of every word he had published, and show that, so far from being guilty of publishing a libel, he had discharged a sacred duty to the public by exposing the utter unfitness of Michael Mulhooly to represent the District from which he is a candidate in the Congress of the United States. We do not now allude to Judge Coke's rulings upon the trial, because a motion for a new trial is pending, and this is not the proper place for its discussion.

"But if Judge Coke's prompt obedience to the message from the Boss—to whom he owes his seat, and to whom he must look for a renomination—in connection with what followed his visit, forces people to believe that Judge Coke is the mere creature of the Ring, and executes its orders under the pretense of administering Justice, Judge Coke has no one but himself to blame; and, being thus suspected, he would show greater wisdom than he has hitherto displayed, if he would at once abandon the judgment-seat before the people drive him from it.

"It is, unfortunately, a matter of common belief that Judge Coke is not the only Judge upon the Bench to-day whom the Ring feels safe in approaching in secret, and instructing in advance about cases to be tried in which its creatures are parties. A Judge who would take a bribe is not more despicable than one who is willing to be thus approached and directed how to administer, not justice, but injustice.

"To all such Judges we now call, Halt! The people will no longer tolerate such infamous practices.

"If Judge Coke thinks we have done him any injustice, we challenge him to call us forthwith to account for this pointed and solemn warning, deliberately given."

No notice was ever taken of this challenge, because its author had been convicted according to law as a common libeler of mankind.

XXI.

One Way to Run a Campaign.

MR. HENRY ARMOR entered upon his campaign in a manner which indicated clearly that he did *not* understand his business.

He did not visit bar-rooms, or drink with and treat the party-workers, or hunt up and consult with the election officers, or endeavor to conciliate the "boys" by promising them appointments. Nor did he call upon the Heads of Departments and seek to induce them to issue orders to their subordinates relative to the amount and kind of work which they were required to do in their respective Election Districts. He probably would have said that a man who would resort to such methods to secure his election to any office was unfit for the office and unworthy of public trust. It is doubtful whether he could have told the name of a single member of the City Committee, or of a President of a Ward Committee in his District.

As he had been nominated by sixty-one out of the ninety-seven delegates, who, according to his belief, should have composed the regular Convention, and had also been regularly nominated by the Reform Association; and as he had subsequently been indorsed by every minister of the gospel and bank president in his District, and by "Thousands of Our Business-men, Taxpayers and Most Respectable, Intelligent, Wealthy, Prominent and Influential Citizens," as he was was informed by the large posters which met his eye at every corner, he considered his election almost a political certainty.

His friends, believing that his eloquence could not fail to convince the voters of his fitness for Congress, organized a series of meetings to be held in each Ward, and made arrangements for a grand ratification meeting to be held at the Academy of Music on the Saturday night immediately preceding the election. At each of these meetings Mr. Armor spoke in his usual scholarly, elegant and eloquent manner. His friends all declared that his speeches were unquestionably the ablest that had ever been made in the city. The *Truth-teller* devoted a full page each morning to these meetings, and published verbatim reports of his speeches. The other newspapers, however, regarding such matters as uninteresting to their readers, disposed of them in something after this fashion:

"The kickers and bolters held a meeting last night at ——— Hall, which was addressed by Henry Armor and others."

Many an ambitious young member of the bar who had devoted weeks to the preparation of a speech which he regarded as a masterpiece of oratory was surprised, on getting out of bed before daylight in anticipation of reading his own polished sentences in print, to find that he, and two or three as distinguished orators as himself, had been bunched like asparagus-sprouts, by some unapprecia-

ONE WAY TO RUN A CAMPAIGN. 175

tive reporter, in that stereotyped phrase, "and others."

No attempt was made by the Committee which was charged with the management of Mr. Armor's campaign to effect any organization of the voters in his interest, beyond the formation of a club in each Ward, called the "Young Men's Reform Association." These clubs were composed of young lawyers, storekeepers and clerks in banks, counting-houses and insurance offices. Each member wore a high silk hat, dark clothes, white gloves and a badge of white satin, upon which was printed in gilt letters the number of the Ward, the name of the association and a peculiar device.

When these five clubs all turned out, parading about two thousand handsome and handsomely dressed young men, they attracted universal admiration, and the ministers of the gospel, bank presidents and "Thousands of Our Business-men, Tax-payers, and Most Respectable, Intelligent, Wealthy, Prominent and Influential Citizens" felt that the country was certainly safe.

On the appointed night the "Grand Ratification Meeting in Favor of Reform and of the Election of Henry Armor, Esq.," was duly held. The Academy of Music was crowded from floor to ceiling and presented a brilliant spectacle. In the middle of the stage, and immediately over the orator's table hung suspended an enormous copy of the old Liberty Bell, around the rim of which appeared the familiar inscription: "PROCLAIM LIBERTY THROUGHOUT ALL THE LAND, UNTO ALL THE INHABITANTS THEREOF." Upon the body of the bell blazed out in dazzling letters of light, formed of innumerable gas-jets, this inscription:—

NO KING

NO CLOWN

SHALL RULE

THIS TOWN.

The front of the stage was crowded with ministers of the gospel, bank presidents and

"Thousands of our Business-men, Taxpayers, and Most Respectable, Intelligent, Wealthy, Prominent and Influential Citizens."

Honorable Ingersole Aspenwall presided, assisted by a large number of Vice-Presidents, whose combined wealth was said to exceed $100,000,000.

When Mr. Armor was introduced the vast audience rose to their feet and gave him a right royal greeting. So great was the enthusiasm that even ladies stood upon the seats waving their handkerchiefs and fans, and some of them, carried away by the novel excitement of the occasion, grew hysterical. Old gray-haired gentlemen on the stage so far forgot themselves that they pounded with their canes and threw up their hats like school-boys. Finally, when he could be heard, Mr. Armor began with these words:

"I do not mistake the meaning of this greeting. It is not merely a compliment to the speaker, or an indorsement of your candidate. It has a deeper significance. It is the death-knell of Boss-rule. It is the shout of victory which a free people sends up over its new declaration of independence. It means that you have resolved from this day forward to govern this city yourselves, without the assistance of any self-appointed Boss, whether native-born or foreign-born."

As each sentence rang out, clear and distinct as the note of a bugle, it was answered by cheer after cheer, to assure the orator that he had read the hearts of his hearers aright and had uttered their sentiments.

He continued:—

"I do not war against individuals. It is not the Boss who happens to be in the ascendancy to-day that I antagonize. It is the Boss of to-day—of to-morrow—of all time who is my enemy; it is the Boss in the City, the Boss in the State, the Boss in the Nation against whom I would have you wage unending war. It is the Boss system which I arraign as the curse of the country and the shame of our age. By this system the public servants are made the masters of the people. By this system the ten thousand employees of the City are made ten thousand arms with which the Boss of the City rules the whole community. By this system the twenty thousand servants of the State are converted into twenty thousand hands with which the Boss of the State holds the commonwealth by the throat. By this system the hundred thousand employees of the Nation become a hundred thousand bonds which the National Bosses bind upon the people of the Nation, converting them into slaves bound to obey their imperial orders.

"The opportunity which it gives a corrupt Boss to plunder the people is one of the least of the many evils which flow from the system. It begets corruption in every branch of the public service, and tempts every man in office to become a thief. It teaches that official dishonesty is no crime—that official perjury is no sin—that to override the will of the people and to trample upon the sanctity of the ballot is the highest duty of American citizenship. It breeds universal corruption, and fosters in the rising generation an utter disregard of law, of morality and of common decency in everything pertaining to politics. It is like that most loathsome of diseases, which creeps from limb to limb, and from individual to individual, until the whole community is a community of lepers. Boss-rule is political leprosy. There can be no political health where it is permitted to exist.

"It cannot be cured; it must be extirpated. There is no remedy which you can apply and say, 'Lo, the sore is healed!' You need not hope to purge your party from it by amending your party rules. You can do that only by purging it of these political lepers, and that can be done only by starving them to death. When honest men learn that they owe a higher duty to their city, their State and their country than they do to their party, they will have found the only antidote for this poison. When they apply this antidote freely at the ballot-box by voting down the political leper and his candidate, the day of deliverance will not be far off. When the independent voter and the scratcher shall have grown so strong that they can and will prevent the election of every unworthy candidate who has managed to secure a nomination, Boss-rule and Ring-rule can be crushed out. They exist only upon the spoils of office, and grow strong only when their party is largely in the majority. Their power is based solely upon the devotion of honest voters to the party. They preach the political religion of 'fidelity to party,' and, like false priests, grow fat upon the fruits of their preaching. The dishonest official whose pockets stand out with his stolen wealth considers it an unpardonable sin for an honest man to scratch his ticket. Fidelity to party, wherever the Boss system exists, is treason to yourself, your country, your God. There is but one true political religion for honest men to practice, and that is to vote for an honest man because he is honest, and to vote against a dishonest man, no matter what party claims him as its candidate—to keep an honest man in office as long as you can, no matter what party put him there, for fear a less honest man may take his place. I believe that the honest citizens in every community outnumber ten to one the class from which Bosses are bred, and when the honest citizens of this country learn this religion and practice it, Boss-rule will be no more."

For nearly two hours the orator continued to delight his audience with such "rhetorical fireworks and political generalities," and, as they had come to hear just such sentiments, they were wrought up to the highest pitch of enthusiasm. When he had finished, every man and woman present insisted upon shaking him by the hand and assuring him of his triumphant election.

That night when he left his club, where a banquet had been given in his honor, he entertained no doubt that he would be elected by several thousand majority.

XXII.

Another Way to Run a Campaign.

HENRY ARMOR, however, was deceived by surface indications. He knew nothing of the power of the Leaders, the Ring and the Boss.

The "I made 'im" is no idle boast, nor is the "I'm fur 'im" an empty promise. The Boss's "I Will" is the Leaders' "We Must," and when they They determine to "make" a man, he is as good as made; when they determine to unmake he is already undone.

The first law of an army is unquestioning, implicit obedience. Not infrequently has the disregard of, or the failure to execute, an apparently trifling military order caused the defeat of a great army—the downfall of an empire—the overthrow of a civilization—the opening of a new volume of the world's history.

The Leaders, the Ring and the Boss command an army composed of elements as dangerous as those which make up the crew of a pirate ship. The instant the slightest sign of weakness is shown, each man aspires to be commander, and is willing to sink the ship and all on board rather than to forego his own ambitious schemes. Therefore, disobedience, or want of obedience, means danger, not only of defeat, disaster and ruin, but also—as the Reformers believe—of the PENITENTIARY. A repulse may prove to be a rout. The loss of a single member of the Municipal Legislature may mean a reorganization—rearrangement of Committees—INVESTIGATION, and—who can tell what? It is imperatively necessary, therefore, that every man shall be taught that to fail is to betray, to disobey is to rebel; and that to do either is to invite political death. Punishment is more than a duty; it is an absolute necessity for self-preservation.

There are also dangers from without as well as from within. The Leaders, the Ring and

THE GENIUS OF THE RING.
"The Boss's 'I Will' is the Leaders' 'We Must.'"—p. 185.

Copyrighted, 1889, by Gebbie & Co.

the Boss are required to practice eternal vigilance. They are compelled to do more than simply to repel hostile assaults; they must punish them with political annihilation. Their power to be preserved must be feared. It must be proved to be even greater to punish than to reward. Therefore, it does not stop at removing an insubordinate from place —withdrawing from a disobedient editor all patronage—placing insurmountable obstacles between a too independent candidate and the object of his ambition; it pursues its victim like a remorseless, an implacable, an inexorable Fate. For those assailants whom such punishments cannot reach, others are provided. What cannot be done directly is done by indirection.

The vengeance of the Leaders, the Ring and the Boss is like the Vendetta which received its name in Corsica, but which was a religion among the ancient Scandinavians, and has been practiced in every age and in every country to redress those wrongs for which the law provides no remedy. Its agencies are as numerous, as secret, as dangerous as those employed to-day by the Nihilists of Russia, or those which were practiced by the Thugs of India prior to 1837. Its punishments even extend to the destruction of private character, the invasion of the family circle, the assault upon womanly honor, and violence to life and limb. Few persons comprehend the power which a single man with a million of dollars can exert, if he will. Fewer still are able to comprehend the terrific power which the Leaders, the Ring and the Boss can wield, when it is necessary to do so, for self-preservation. In every large city is to be found a class of men who form their secret police, executing Their will without fear, knowing that They stand as a shield between Their agents and the law. If the secrets of the "mysterious disappearances" of which we read were all disclosed—but fortunately, perhaps, the dead cannot speak.

Henry Armor not only failed to understand the power of the Leaders, the Ring and the Boss, against which he hurled his polished and not wholly harmless sentences, but he also failed to comprehend the necessity which demanded his defeat. The contest, owing to the tendency of the people to run to extremes, had assumed so serious a shape that it rendered doubtful the election of three, and possibly of five candidates for the Municipal Legislature in that Congressional District. The Reform assault, therefore, threatened not only to drive in the line of skirmishers, but also to endanger the safety of Their whole army, and made the overthrow of Their empire possible. The ascendency of the Reform Association, at all events, meant a standing menace to the power and safety of the Leaders, the Ring and the Boss, and, therefore, They said, "We must destroy them to save Ourselves." It was the *delenda est Carthago* of the Romans.

The Leaders, the Ring and the Boss were not idle. They also held meetings—not to make converts, but to encourage the rank and file, and to conceal the manner in which Their skirmishers, Their sharp-shooters, Their guerillas, Their bush-whackers and Their light-cavalry were engaged, and the mode in which They had determined to handle Their troops and give battle.

Neither Michael Mulhooly, nor Blossom Brick, nor the Boss spoke at any of these meetings. Their time and talents were more usefully employed. They were wholly occupied in strengthening Their wavering lines; in compelling submission where They discovered signs of insubordination; in exhausting the possibilities of each Department; in laying out the exact work expected of each one of the many hundreds of employees in the District, and in arranging all those countless details with election officers, window-book men and committees to bring out the vote, which go so far, in every close contest, towards conquering success.

One of the first steps which was taken was to make an example of those employees of Departments not directly under Their control, who had been led into acting with the Reform Association, by reason of its professed respectability, and by the plausible argument that, as Henry Armor was a candidate of the party, although an independent one, he could be supported by every party-man without infidelity to the party. Against such offenders They acted promptly and decidedly.

Henry White, a clerk in the Department of the State Treasury, was one of the first victims. He had paraded with the Reform Association of his Ward, and had acted at a public meeting of the Association as one of the secretaries, and had read a series of resolutions strongly indorsing Henry Armor, and, of course, by implication condemning the Boss. He had not been long enough in office to know any better.

His offense was a glaring one, and nothing but his official head would appease the wrath which he had unconsciously aroused. Accordingly the Boss called promptly upon the Head of the Department—made known His will—refused to take a denial or listen to an apology, saying only "I'll tache 'im," and as He could not be offended with impunity, although the Department was not under His control, that very afternoon Mr. White, on leaving the office, received an official envelope which he discovered contained a written notice of his dismissal. It was a thunderbolt from a cloudless sky. He had just taken a small house and furnished it, mainly on credit, and was daily expecting his young wife to be confined with her first baby. He read the letter over again and again, seeking in vain to find some explanation of his offense, in the lines which told only too plainly of his punishment. With a heavy heart he sat down at the supper-table which she had prepared, according to her custom, to welcome him after his day's work, and pleaded a headache as an excuse for the depression which he could not wholly conceal from the watchful eyes of the poor little woman to whom he was lover, hero, and almost God.

That night, while sleep made many another aching heart temporarily forget its woes, she refused to him her blessed consolation. He heard the solemn tones of the great townclock slowly counting off the hours of the long night. He listened impatiently to his own cheap clock ticking away, one by one, the seconds, each one of which brought him one step nearer the moment when he could meet his Chief face to face, and demand an explanation of this heavy punishment for a fault of which he was ignorant. He looked at his young wife, sleeping in blissful ignorance of the great trouble which the next day's sun would surely disclose, dreaming of the baby that was so soon, like a kind message from the Great Father, to gladden their humble but happy home; and then the silent, scalding-hot tears one by one—but, Pshaw! why waste any sympathy upon a fool who expected to live by a system which he was not willing to obey as a slave?

Of course he thought when morning came that in that one night he had lived through ten years of misery. Of course he hurried to the Department, still hoping that the God to whom he prayed for his wife and unborn child, might find some means of arresting the calamity. Of course the ostensible Chief of the Department received him kindly, and explained to him the crime which he had committed, and expressed his regret that he had been compelled to thus summarily dismiss him. Of course he grew indignant at this, his first lesson in practical politics, and denounced his dismissal as an act of tyranny, wicked, disgraceful and cruel; and then, suddenly thinking of his home, of his wife, and of how he was to provide food and nursing and a doctor, broke down utterly, and, sobbing like a child, told of his great necessities, and promised to submit in the future and to do anything in his power to repair the wrong he had done, and was told, kindly but frankly, that nothing could be done, as his place had already been filled. Of course he went away cursing the system, and praying God to visit upon the Boss something of the misery which He caused others to suffer, and stopping every acquaintance whom he met on the street to tell his story, receiving sympathy from all, and from some the consoling assurance that he " ought not to have been such a d——d fool." Of course some of his hearers, warned by his example, endeavored to make amends for their own indiscretions by going from one saloon to another where there was a prospect of meeting any of the Leaders, and

ANOTHER WAY TO RUN A CAMPAIGN. 193

hurrahing for "Mulhooly all the time." Of course, when he was at last compelled to go home, tired, hungry, and sick at heart, and to tell his poor young wife all, the shock brought on—— Well, Nature has not provided us with a sufficient supply of tears to meet the demands made upon our sensibilities by the miseries brought upon the innocent and helpless by the follies of our fellow-men.

A few such examples are sufficient to strike terror to the hearts, not only of the employees of the Leaders, the Ring and the Boss, but also of all who are in the public service and whom Their vengeance can possibly reach.

Their next task was to raise sufficient money to defray the expense of electing Michael Mulhooly, and it was an easy one.

Henry Armor, indorsed as he was by bank-presidents and millionaires, who, according to their own views, had contributed most liberally to his campaign fund, would have been greatly astonished had he been told that a sum nearly three times as large as that which had been subscribed by his wealthy friends had been raised without difficulty to secure his defeat.

Blossom Brick, as Chairman of a sub-Committee of the City Committee, took upon himself the, to him, agreeable duty of collecting this fund. Lists were always ready for use on such occasions, containing the name of every man directly or indirectly employed under the city government, with the amount of his salary, or an estimate of the Rebates and *aliunde* profits attached to his office, set opposite his name.

It was customary to levy an assessment varying from one to five per cent. upon the estimated salary of each. With a salary list of $6,595,625, one per cent. of this sum would amount to $65,956. Even if but two-thirds of those who were requested to pay their assessments responded—and it is a dangerous thing for any man to refuse to comply with so obviously just a request—over $40,000 could thus be raised in a few days. Allowing a proper percentage of this sum for natural leakage while passing through the hands of those charged with its collection—and surely those who labor day and night for the party without any ostensible salary ought not to be expected to account for every cent—it will be readily seen that if Blossom Brick's rule for estimating the cost of securing an election be correct, there still would remain a very large sum to be used in making the requisite number of election officers "solid."

In this rule Blossom Brick placed implicit faith. He laughed when other people talked about relying upon public meetings and speeches to carry an election, and repeated one of his favorite expressions, "*An election officer well in hand is worth a score of voters on the half shell.*"

Having raised this fund, he also took upon himself the, to him, agreeable duty of disbursing it. One of his peculiarities in managing this responsible part of the campaign, for which he was noted, was that he never allowed any portion of such a fund to remain unexpended, or turned over any surplus to the Committee for a reserve fund. On the contrary, he invariably had bills outstanding, and claims of his own for bills which he had felt compelled to pay out of his own pocket. This proved how thoroughly he did his work.

Upon him also mainly devolved the delicate and responsible duty of conducting those diplomatic negotiations, not only with election officers, upon whom he so strongly relied, but also with that valuable body of statesmen, such as Hon. Hugh McCann, Piggy Degan and Pud. Muldoon, who have a positive genius for bringing out voters, even in Wards in which they do not reside, and where they are supposed to have no very extended acquaintance. It is sufficient to say that when such work was done by Blossom Brick it was well done, and that he highly commended Michael Mulhooly for the assistance which he rendered in more than one case of peculiar delicacy and difficulty.

Each Election District was carefully and accurately canvassed, and at a private meeting of the Leaders, the Ring and the Boss, held on the Saturday evening when Mr. Henry Armor was delighting the large audience in the Academy of Music with his rhetorical display, They were able to point out exactly the amount and character of work which was still necessary to be done in certain Election Districts to insure success.

On the night before the election—so admirably had Michael Mulhooly's campaign been managed—the sporting men commenced to bet heavily on his election.

XXIII.

The Result.

AT ten o'clock on election morning it was evident that Henry Armor was polling an exceedingly strong vote. At two o'clock P. M. bets of $1,000 to $500 that his majority would not be less than two thousand were offered at the clubs without takers. At four o'clock P. M. the afternoon papers published reports of disturbances at several voting places in the District.

When the polls closed there seemed to be no doubt of the election of the Reform Candidate, but by a much smaller majority than his friends had predicted. For the last hour, in a number of Election Districts, the Mulhooly voters rallied in such strength and numbers around the polls as to prevent any other voters from approaching the window.

THE RESULT.

Toward nine o'clock P. M. rumors commenced to come in of frauds in counting the returns, and of the carrying off of ballot-boxes by bodies of armed men who declared that the Armor election officers contemplated making false returns in favor of their candidate. In one of these Election Districts an election officer was shot, and in another two citizens who were assisting the election officers to defend the ballot-boxes were reported to have been mortally wounded.

At two o'clock A. M. a number of Election Districts were yet to be heard from, no returns having been made, owing, as was alleged by Michael Mulhooly's friends, to the attempt of a body of armed roughs in Armor's employ to count their candidate in.

Michael Mulhooly and Blossom Brick were up all night, driving from one voting-place to another, encouraging their election officers to stand firm, and not to allow Mulhooly *to be counted out*.

At daylight Blossom Brick ordered Patsy Maguire—at whose saloon they had just arrived, worn out by their arduous labors—to open a basket of wine, and invited up some twenty members of the "Michael Mulhooly Campaign Club"—who had also been engaged all night in guarding the sanctity of the ballot—to drink to the health of their "next Congressman, Hon. Michael Mulhooly."

When the official returns were all in and counted it was found that, notwithstanding the unprecedented frauds which were alleged to have been committed in the interest of the Reform candidate, Michael Mulhooly was elected by a majority of three hundred and seventy-nine votes, and consequently, he received the certificate of election.

Thus were the Leaders, the Ring and the Boss vindicated by the people.

Mr. Armor's friends were astonished at the result, and indignantly denied the charges of fraud made against them. They claimed that their candidate had been elected by more than one thousand majority, and had been deliberately counted out.

Steps were immediately taken to contest Michael Mulhooly's seat. A committee was appointed to canvass the Congressional District; a large fund was subscribed to defray the necessary expenses, and a number of eminent counsel were employed to prepare the proper petition and present the case at the opening of the next session of Congress.

The *Truth-teller* from day to day published the details, which it claimed would establish the most wicked and stupendous scheme to over-ride the will of the people that had ever been perpetrated or attempted in the city.

A number of election officers were arrested and held to bail, and one of them made an affidavit that he had been paid $150 by Blossom Brick, in the presence of Michael Mulhooly, to alter the returns so that they would show a gain of fifty votes for Mulhooly. It was announced that upon this affidavit a warrant would be issued for the arrest of both these gentlemen, but no such warrant was issued, on account of the sudden disappearance of the man who had made this affidavit. This singular conduct on his part gave color to the allegation of Blossom Brick that it was only a "put-up job," and that the man had been paid by Armor's friends to make the affidavit and then "skip," so as to enable them to cover up their own frauds.

As the session of Congress drew near, each party claimed to have secured overwhelming evidences of frauds committed by the other side. The contest, however, was never to be made, owing to the sudden death of Mr. Henry Armor, who, notwithstanding his peculiar political views, had won the regard and esteem of many of the best people in the community, by whom his loss was sincerely mourned.

The night before Michael Mulhooly's departure to take his seat in the American Congress the Michael Mulhooly Campaign Clubs tendered him a serenade and made a street parade, marshalled by Hon. Hugh McCann, Piggy Degan and Pud. Muldoon, and carrying transparencies upon which were inscribed various striking and original mottoes.

Two of these transparencies, borne side by side, were so peculiar and suggestive, that this sketch of a distinguished representative

PRACTICE *VS.* THEORY.—p. 203.

Copyrighted, 1889, by Gebbie & Co.

of the system which will fill so important a page of the political history of the country, cannot be more fittingly concluded than by reproducing the mottoes which they bore:

MIKE MULHOOLY, M. C. BY THE GRACE OF THE GODS.	A GOVERNMENT OF THE PEOPLE, BY THE PEOPLE, AND FOR THE PEOPLE.

The Leaders, the Ring, and the Boss, and Their thousands of dependants, had been truly—*Solid for Mulhooly.*

APPENDIX.

DADDY RAT AS JAIL-KEEPER.

[From the Baltimore *Civil Service Reformer*, September, 1888.]

WHEN James Ratcliffe, otherwise "Daddy Rat," is brought out of the old Tolbooth, or "Heart of Midlothian," and calmly proposes that, instead of being hanged on this his fourth sentence, he shall be made under-turnkey, the magistrate is appalled at the fellow's effrontery. A strange set of circumstances lead (in the story) to the granting of his request, and Madge Wildfire meets her new jailer with the salutation, "Gude e'en to ye, Daddy Ratton; they tauld me ye were hanged, man." In relating this incident, Sir Walter Scott probably thought that he had driven the improbable quite as far as was safe, even in a novel. Truth, however, is stranger than fiction; at least it is so in the State of Maryland. Had Scott lived here in the present year of our Lord, he would have found that what he considered a rather sensational episode was the "regular" rule, and our penal institutions were in great measure intrusted to men of known criminal antecedents. At this very hour Mr. Mike Murphy, one of the most notorious of the Weyler gang, is deputy warden in the Baltimore City Jail, in which he was a convict only a few years ago. He took the place of Dick Carter, Weyler's brother-in-law, and another of the same gang, whose record shows thirteen arrests and three indictments, and who retired to assume the charge of Weyler's saloon at the Cross Street Market, which is the rendezvous of the gang.

But the most sensational appointment we have yet had was made a few weeks ago, when John W. Weyler himself, the veritable " Daddy Rat " of the organization, was appointed Warden of the Penitentiary, the institution in which two of his most useful followers, Burke and Kennedy, are now serving out sentences for a political murder. Is not this a little startling, even for Baltimore? Does not the presence of three members of this gang in important places in the management of our jail and penitentiary give to the direction of those institutions rather too much the air of a representative government?

The rise of this man Weyler is the strongest of all proofs of the close connection of our "regular" organization with our criminal population. Weyler has for some time been a prominent and a corrupt member of the City Council, and is now the President of the First Branch, and is sometimes Acting Mayor. The giving to him, however, of the important office of Warden of the Penitentiary at the same time that he holds these other positions, is an unusual proceeding, and deserves attention. Let us see who and what Weyler is. It is a little difficult to give a clear notion of this. The simple method of getting at the record of an ordinary Baltimore

APPENDIX.

"statesman" will not do in this case. A short run through the dockets of the Criminal Court will give for most of our rulers a history both satisfactory and voluminous. Weyler, however, was a detective at the beginning of his career, has all of Daddy Rat's wariness, keeps dark when sober, and generally acts on the detective's rule to do nothing in person that can be done by an agent. His life, therefore, is not "spread upon the records" as are those of so many of our great men.

One instance will serve to illustrate this difference. In the congressional election of 1880 Weyler had had appointed as judges of election his friend "Mike" Murphy and a young man named Bowers, a sailor, scarcely of age, entirely ignorant of all election matters and fresh from his first voyage—the recognized machinery for stuffing a ballot-box, namely, one scamp and one tyro. Acting under instructions from Weyler as to his powers and duties as judge, Bowers refused admittance to and assaulted the United States Marshal. For this Bowers was convicted in the United States Court and served a short term in jail, but Weyler escaped all punishment. Usually working thus by indirection, it is difficult to fasten his crimes upon him. Some facts can, however, be given that will illustrate his true character and show the enormity of his appointment to so important a post as that of Warden of the Penitentiary. The most significant of these is that Weyler is chief of the Seventeenth Ward gang, that has figured so prominently in the discussions and disgraces of the last two years. He has the distribution of the patronage, and selects the agents that are needed for the

APPENDIX. 207

kind of work on which "the party" relies in that ward. The names of his principal lieutenants and agents have become familiar; but, at the risk of telling an old story, we will recall a few of them, as showing what kind of an organization Weyler is at the head of:

James F. Busey is Superintendent of Streets. Has been arrested thirty-nine times and indicted twelve times. (Said by Mayor Hodges to have "an interesting family.") Many of his indictments have been for very brutal assaults, and one at least for an assault on a woman. Busey was once Weyler's senior officer, but Weyler has been promoted over him for meritorious service.

Beauregard Carter, a notorious and dangerous ruffian, killed in cold blood by other members of the gang some four years ago.

Tom Hogan, indicted for the killing of Councilman Mulligan, but acquitted.

John Burke and James Kennedy are now serving out a term in the penitentiary for the murder of John F. Curran. They were appointed judges of election through the Weyler machinery, and this was their first act after they joined the harmonious officialty described by Mayor Hodges.

Richard Carter was until a few weeks ago Deputy Warden at the jail. He has been arrested thirteen times and indicted three times. He is now in charge of the groggery, No. 25 Weyler Street, formerly kept and still owned by Weyler himself, which is the meeting place of the "officialty" of the ward. He is Weyler's brother-in-law. A good photograph of this gentleman would be of much use during our local campaigns, and during off years it would serve as an illustration for Dickens' character of Bill Sykes.

Mike Murphy is now a Deputy Warden at the jail. He was formerly a convict there. He has often been arrested. For many years he was an assistant to Jim Busey, but he took Carter's place at the jail when the latter took charge of Weyler's saloon. As the Hatter said to the March Hare, "All move up one place."

John Murphy, *alias* Butch, is a well-known tough, frequently arrested, and always in office. He is the close friend and protégé of Weyler, who has for years kept him in his present post of page in the City Council. He is under indictment at the present time for fraudulent registration.

As to Weyler's own individual character, much is known, but not much is speakable. A few of the more presentable facts will, however, prove interesting. He was once on the police detective force, but was dismissed for misconduct. Weyler was arrested in 1884 for intimidating voters. The charge was not pressed, for the reason that the prosecuting witness was unwilling to press it. This reason, when entered in political cases, generally means that the prosecuting witness was threatened or bought off by the accused and his friends.

Characteristic of his associations are the thrashings Weyler has suffered. He was beaten in a very brutal way in his own bar-room some years ago by one "Billy" Carroll, a brother of James F. Busey, who for some reason had had his name changed. He was also beaten by one

Michael Wagner in front of the saloon of the well-known ex-City Councilman Jacob Crow, and was picked up in an unconscious state from that statesman's cellar-door. The latest episode of this sort in Weyler's career, however, was the assault upon him in 1884 by " Bill " Harig, a well-known political "bruiser" of the Fifteenth Ward, who for years back has been equally at home in the criminal dock and at the governmental table. Harig assaulted Weyler most viciously, apparently without any provocation. He was indicted for assault with intent to kill, but he was only convicted of a common assault. Harig exhibited during the trial the most reckless audacity, and rather interested the jury in spite of the evident fact that he was a desperado. He called as witnesses indiscriminately the most prominent and respectable men in Weyler's ward to prove that he was not to be believed on oath, and Weyler made no attempt to controvert this charge. Harig boasted openly that he had gotten himself arrested for the sake of producing this proof, and his character and behavior make this seem not improbable.

These are a few facts in the life of this man who is now President of the First Branch of the City Council, who sometimes acts as Mayor, and who has been appointed Warden of our Penitentiary. They will serve to show in a very general way the style of man chosen for this place. We have not gone into the more revolting details of his life, because to do so would make this recital too disgusting.

People will ask how such a man can get an office of

responsibility like the wardenship of the penitentiary? But it should be understood that Weyler, in spite of his low character, is quite a power in our city politics. Mr. Rasin's three principal lieutenants in the city are Quinn, Mahon, and John F. Weyler; and it is said that Weyler of late has had more influence than either of the others. With two of the best offices in the city, his seat at the governmental table is a very prominent one, and he is no man to go unfed. The post of Warden is a particularly attractive one to a covetous statesman, as it affords among its perquisites free board and lodging in a fine house and unlimited "supplies." There is a peculiar significance, too, in Weyler's appointment, which is apparent on reflection. It seems likely that all political offenders are to be granted clemency as soon as it shall be safe. A large part of the convicted judges and clerks have already been pardoned by Governor Jackson, and the last legislature condoned the crimes of all not yet convicted. But the pardon of Burke and Kennedy, who rendered a more important service than any of the other judges, is still delayed, doubtless, as Higgins said when trying to get rid of one of the witnesses against them, till public attention shall "blow over." The two martyrs have a right to consider themselves most unfairly and ungratefully treated. It cannot be doubted that they are restless and complaining. Is it uncharitable to surmise that one of the duties of the chief of the Seventeenth Ward organization, who has been put in charge of them, will be to keep them from "squealing" till the city statesmen can compel the Governor to pardon them?